SUPER-EASY EXCEL GUIDE 2025

The Complete Step-by-Step Guide to Mastering Excel in Just 5 Days—With Practical Exercises, Time-Saving Shortcuts, and Automation Tricks to Work Smarter and Get Ahead!

Anthony Salvage

TABLE OF CONTENTS

CHAPTER 1: EXCEL BASICS & NAVIGATION

Welcome to your first day with Excel, a tool that can often seem daunting to newcomers but holds the keys to transforming how you work, analyze, and present data in your professional and personal life. We begin our journey at the very foundation—Excel basics and navigation. Consider this chapter as your friendly tour guide into the world of spreadsheets, where instead of feeling overwhelmed, you'll gain a solid foothold, pleased with each step advancing you forward.

Imagine walking into a giant, well-organized library where every book could reveal secrets to smarter and faster decisions, if only you knew where to find them. That's Excel for you! To start, we'll explore the different 'sections' of this library—the Ribbon, cells, and sheets. Each component in Excel is designed to make data storage, access, and processing intuitive. Think of the Ribbon as the master index where every processing tool and feature you need is cataloged. Cells and sheets? They're your individual books and shelves, storing each piece of your data effectively.

Tailoring Excel to boost your efficiency from the get-go is akin to setting up your workspace. We'll tweak the Quick Access Toolbar and discover shortcuts that feel almost like having secret passages in our metaphorical library, allowing you to reach your results quicker than you'd expect.

Lastly, the quintessential skills of saving, exporting, and sharing workbooks will ensure that your work doesn't just stay on your computer. Like lending a well-organized notebook full of insights, sharing workbooks helps you collaborate and make an impact in your team or across your network. As we progress, remember this day is about building comfort and familiarity, layering the basic bricks to construct your fluency in Excel. Each concept we'll cover is a stepping stone to more advanced tools and tricks awaiting you in the days to come. By the end of today, you'll not only navigate through Excel with more confidence but also customize it like a personal workspace that's both efficient and intuitive. So let's turn the page and start this empowering journey together!

WHAT IS EXCEL? A BEGINNER'S INTRODUCTION

Picture yourself in the early 1980s—an era of big hair, bold fashions, and the birth of a tool that would revolutionize the way the world managed data. This tool, Microsoft Excel, started as a simple idea: to help people organize and manipulate data easily on their personal computers. As part of the larger Microsoft Office suite, Excel was designed from the onset to be user-friendly—a spreadsheet application that could perform complex calculations, analyze data, and display information in ways that were visually appealing and easy to understand.

In its nascent form, Excel came to life to fulfill the needs of accountants and businessmen who were drowning in data analysis performed manually or using limited software capabilities.

Excel offered them a lifeline—a grid interface composed of rows and columns where data could be easily entered, stored, and configured.

Through the decades, Excel evolved, growing in sophistication and capabilities. From the introduction of graphical tools and PivotTables in the early versions to the integration of powerful analytics in later versions, each iteration of Excel has built upon the last, making it not only a tool for financial experts but for anyone needing to manage data, from scientists to students, marketers to medical professionals.

When we unpack what Excel really is, we see it as a vast, versatile toolkit. It comprises a grid of cells, with each cell able to contain data, be it text, a number, or a formula. Formulas are fundamental to Excel's utility, letting you perform calculations or manipulate the contents of other cells. Moreover, Excel's function library is expansive, capable of handling financial, statistical, and mathematical calculations, among others.

Data visualization is another cornerstone of Excel, with features that allow users to create a wide variety of charts and graphs from the data entered in the worksheets—transforming raw numbers into impactful visual stories. This capability makes it an invaluable tool for those presenting data and needing to make an impact on their audience.

Excel also comes with features like sorting and filtering, which allow you to manage large datasets, making it easier to focus on the information that matters most. The introduction of PivotTables was a significant leap forward, providing the ability to dynamically arrange and summarize data, which helps in identifying trends and making quick decisions.

Automation through macros and later, the introduction of Visual Basic for Applications (VBA), turned repetitive tasks and complex sequence actions into simple executions. These functionalities, especially when customized, can significantly boost productivity, reducing hours of work to mere minutes through automation.

While discussing Excel, it's also essential to mention its ability to integrate with other software, especially within the Microsoft Office suite. This capability allows for seamless data import and export between tools like Word or PowerPoint, facilitating a more fluid workflow across tasks that require multi-facet data utilization.

In the most recent versions, Excel has embraced cloud computing, reflecting a shift in how data is stored and accessed in an increasingly connected world. With Office 365, Excel has become more than just a desktop application; it is a comprehensive, collaborative platform that allows users to work on datasets in real time, share insights instantly, and access their work from anywhere in the world.

Another leap has been the integration of AI capabilities, which have begun to change how data is analyzed and processed. These AI features can perform complex analyses, recognize patterns, and even predict trends based on historical data, which can be a game-changer in many professional fields.

Through this evolution, Excel has maintained a core promise—to make data handling and decision-making easier. For beginners, starting with Excel can still be as simple as entering data into cells and using basic formulas like SUM or AVERAGE. However, as users' confidence grows, they can delve into more sophisticated features, gradually climbing the ladder of Excel proficiency. The essence of learning Excel in this structured, step-by-step manner within this book is to build a solid foundation—one where understanding grows, skills are sharpened, and possibilities expand. Whether you're aiming for career advancement, seeking to enhance academic work, or managing personal projects, Excel offers tools that go beyond mere number crunching to help you analyze and visualize data in powerful, more insightful ways.

By the end of this journey, Excel will no longer be just a software tool you use; it will be an essential skill you leverage, enhancing your ability to think, analyze, and present data creatively and efficiently. Let's take this step-by-step path towards mastering Excel, breaking down complex functions into understandable chunks, applying practical tips, and using real-world examples to cement your understanding and skills in this powerful tool.

EXPLORING THE INTERFACE: RIBBONS, CELLS, AND SHEETS

When you first open Excel, you might feel like an explorer stepping into an unfamiliar landscape. There's quite a lot to see and do, from navigating mysterious ribbons to managing the cells and sheets that will soon become the bedrock of all your data storytelling. Let's walk through the key features of the Excel interface together, breaking down their functionality in a way that will feel like second nature by the time we're done.

Exploring the Ribbon

The Ribbon in Excel acts like a control panel, neatly organizing tools and options into a series of tabs at the top of your screen. It's your command center, quick to reach and easy to navigate once you understand the logic behind its layout.

Each tab on the Ribbon is grouped by related tasks—be it inserting elements, laying out your page, or reviewing your work. When you click on a tab, such as 'Home', 'Insert', or 'Data', a panel of related tools and features displays, offering everything you need for that specific aspect of your workbook's creation or revision.

For starters, the 'Home' tab contains the most frequently used commands, such as font formatting, cell alignment, number formatting, and conditional formatting. It's your go-to for daily tasks and quick changes. As you grow more comfortable, you'll begin exploring more specialized tabs that cater to more complex operations, such as 'Formulas' for managing mathematical functions or 'Data' for handling complex datasets.

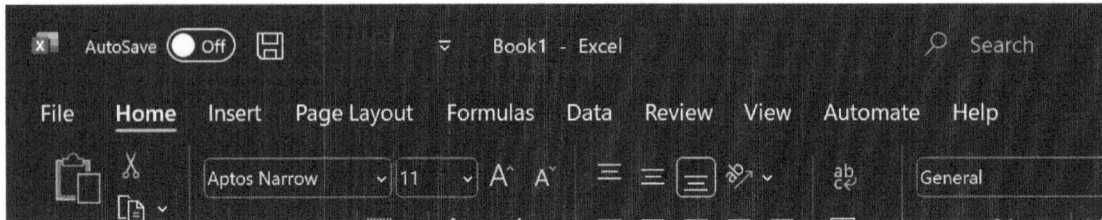

Navigating Cells

Each tiny rectangle in an Excel spreadsheet is called a cell. Think of cells as individual bites of data, the basic building blocks of your spreadsheets. Each cell can be uniquely identified by its address, a combination of its column letter and row number. For instance, the cell in the third column and the fifth row is cell C5. By understanding cell addresses, you can quickly navigate around your spreadsheet or instruct Excel on where to find or place data.

Cells are incredibly versatile: they can contain data, such as text and numbers, or formulas that calculate values using data stored in other cells. When clicked, a cell becomes active, highlighted with a border, ready for you to enter or edit information.

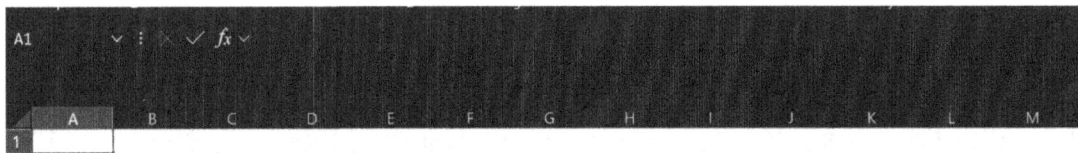

Understanding Sheets

If cells are the pages of your book, then sheets are the chapters. Each Excel file, known as a workbook, can contain multiple sheets, accessible via tabs at the bottom of the window. You can easily add more sheets depending on your needs or move between sheets to manage different kinds of information within the same workbook.

Sheets can be renamed by right-clicking on their tab and selecting 'Rename'. This feature is particularly handy when managing multiple datasets or scenarios in a single workbook, allowing you to keep your workspace organized and intuitive. For example, a budget workbook might have separate sheets labeled 'Income', 'Expenses', and 'Summary' to help navigate through these sections easily.

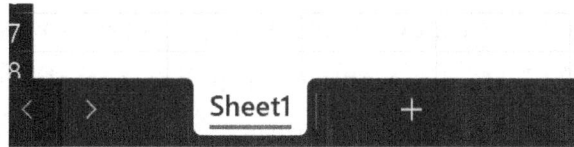

Customization for Efficiency

Excel allows you to customize your workspace for enhanced efficiency. This is particularly useful if you find yourself repeatedly using certain features that aren't readily accessible on the default Ribbon. By customizing the Ribbon, you can add, remove, or rearrange tabs and commands to fit your workflow. Similarly, the Quick Access Toolbar at the top can be customized to include shortcuts to your most-used commands, no matter which tab you are currently using in the Ribbon.

To customize, right-click on the Ribbon and choose 'Customize the Ribbon' to open a dialog box where you can make adjustments according to your preferences and work habits. This makes Excel not just a tool, but *your* tool, molded to your way of working.

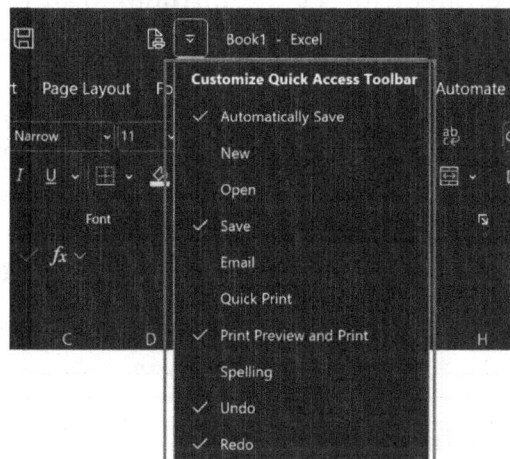

Navigating and Working Efficiently

Knowing a few navigation tricks can also save you a lot of time. For instance, using arrow keys to move between cells is straightforward, but did you know that pressing 'Ctrl' along with an arrow key jumps to the edge of the data in that direction? Such shortcuts can turn tedious tasks into quick actions.

In sum, gaining fluency in navigating the Excel interface is akin to learning the grammar of a new language. Once you understand how to use the Ribbon, manage cells, and organize sheets effectively, you're well on your way to leveraging the full power of Excel. Whether you're balancing budgets, organizing large datasets, or creating complex reports, these skills form the foundation of all your Excel endeavors, turning the unfamiliar landscape into a mapped-out territory you can navigate with confidence.

As we progress further, remember that each of these elements works not just in isolation but in synergy. Excel's power lies not just in its features but in how seamlessly they integrate to turn raw data into compelling stories and insightful analyses. So, take this foundational knowledge and build upon it as we delve deeper into more intricate functionalities of Excel.

CUSTOMIZING EXCEL FOR EFFICIENCY (SHORTCUTS, QUICK ACCESS TOOLBAR)

As you embark on your journey through Excel, one fundamental truth to embrace is this: customization is not just a luxury; it's a necessity for efficiency. The more you mold Excel to fit your workflow, the more time you'll save, and the more effectively you'll work. This section is about turning Excel from a powerful software into a personal assistant that knows exactly what you need and keeps everything you use regularly right at your fingertips.

Harnessing the Power of Shortcuts

Human memory is quirky. We might forget the birthday of a close friend but remember the shortcut key to our favorite Excel function. Why? Because these little shortcuts transform lengthy processes into a button press, streamlining our work and reducing repetitive strain. Excel offers myriad shortcuts, but let's focus on a few key ones that will drastically reduce the number of clicks you make in a day.

For starters, mastering the basics such as Ctrl + C for copy, Ctrl + V for paste, and Ctrl + Z for undo can be game changers. But Excel's specialty lies in those specific shortcuts that handle data like a pro:

- Ctrl + Arrow key: This jumps the cursor to the edge of the data region in a worksheet, speeding up navigation immensely.
- Alt + E, S, V: A classic sequence to paste values only, which strips out formulas and formatting, keeping the data clean.
- Ctrl + Shift + L: Instantly toggles filters on and off from your data ranges, which is pivotal for quick data analysis.

As you get more accustomed to these, incorporate more advanced shortcuts, like creating charts with Alt + F1 or opening the VLOOKUP wizard with Alt + A, V. The idea is to build a repertoire of shortcuts tailored to the tasks you find yourself doing frequently.

Optimizing the Quick Access Toolbar

The Quick Access Toolbar is that tiny strip of icons at the top of Excel, and it's your canvas to create a shortcut masterpiece. By default, it includes save, undo, and redo, but its true potential is realized when you customize it.

To add your most used commands to the Quick Access Toolbar:

1. Right-click on any Ribbon command you frequently use.
2. Select "Add to Quick Access Toolbar."
3. Alternatively, explore more options by clicking on the small dropdown arrow next to the Quick Access Toolbar and selecting "More Commands." Here, you can add a plethora of tools from all categories.

Think of tasks you perform regularly. Do you often freeze panes to keep your header visible while scrolling? Add it to your Quick Access Toolbar. Constantly formatting cells? Add the Format Painter or Cell Style commands for quicker access. The goal is to minimize the distance your mouse travels and reduce the number of clicks, which speeds up your work significantly.

Customizing the Ribbon for a Tailored Experience

The Ribbon is fully customizable and realizing this can transform your workflow. By tailoring the Ribbon, you not only keep necessary tools visible and unnecessary ones out of sight but also group your most used features in a way that reflects how you work.

To customize the Ribbon:

1. Right-click on the Ribbon and select "Customize the Ribbon."
2. In the dialog box that appears, you can rename tabs, add new tabs, or remove existing ones.
3. You can also reorganize commands within the tabs, adding or removing groups to suit your workflow.

Imagine you're working extensively with data analysis—create a tab named 'Data Analysis' and add tools like PivotTables, Chart commands, or anything relevant to your needs. This personalized setup means less time searching through menus and more time doing meaningful work.

Leveraging Excel Options for Personalized Settings

Beyond shortcuts and toolbar adjustments, diving into Excel's options can further enhance your user experience. Access these by clicking on 'File' then 'Options'. Here, you can adjust Excel's behavior to suit your preferences. For instance:

- Set up default fonts and number formats.
- Customize how Excel handles correction and calculation.

- Adjust the view to reduce eye strain or accommodate different screen setups.

Each of these configurations helps tailor Excel to behave in a way that aligns with your expectations and needs, ensuring a smoother workflow.

Practical Application and Flexibility

As you set up your shortcuts, Quick Access Toolbar, and Ribbon, remember: what works excellently for one might not suit another. The beauty of Excel is its flexibility, so experiment with different setups until you find the combination that feels effortless. As your tasks evolve, so should your setup. Reevaluate periodically and make adjustments as your needs change.

In sum, customizing Excel isn't just about making it faster; it's about making it yours. It's about creating an environment where the tools you need are always within easy reach, and the workflow is streamlined to support your daily tasks efficiently. With these customizations, Excel becomes less of a software application and more of a personal work companion, ready to tackle the next data challenge with you. Walkthrough these steps, implement changes tailored to your needs, and watch as Excel's efficiency dramatically transforms your productivity.

SAVING, EXPORTING, AND SHARING WORKBOOKS

As you accumulate data, insights, and beautifully formatted reports in Excel, a natural next step is to ensure your work is not only saved securely but can also be shared and utilized in various formats depending on the need.

In this section, we'll explore how to efficiently manage saving, exporting, and sharing your Excel workbooks, turning these seemingly routine tasks into powerful tools that extend the reach and utility of your efforts.

Saving Your Work: More Than Just a Click

When you think about saving your work in Excel, it might seem straightforward—hit the save icon or press Ctrl+S, and you're set. However, developing a good strategy for saving your work involves more than just periodic saving. This is about ensuring that your data is not only saved but also organized in a way that enhances accessibility and security.

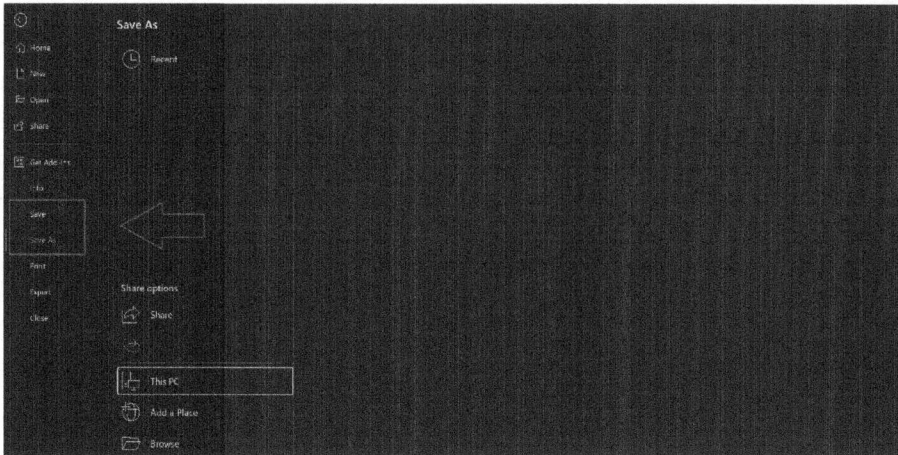

Choosing the Right Format

Excel offers several formats for saving your workbooks, each serving different purposes:

- **XLSX**: The default file format for newer versions of Excel, supporting features like formulas, charts, and macros. It's ideal for everyday use where you need to preserve the full functionality of Excel.

- **XLSM**: If your workbook includes macros, saving it in this format ensures that they run smoothly without security hitches.

- **CSV (Comma Delimited)**: When your data needs to be ported into another program or shared with systems that do not support Excel, CSV is the format of choice. It strips out formatting and formulas, leaving plain text separated by commas.

- **PDF**: Perfect for when you need to share a static version of your sheets that cannot be easily altered. Saving as PDF preserves your layout and formatting, making it ideal for reports and presentations.

AutoSave and Recovery

Excel's AutoSave is a lifesaver, especially when working on complex documents, as it automatically saves your changes to the cloud (if you're using OneDrive or SharePoint) or to your specified directory at regular intervals. Ensure this feature is turned on by default via File > Options > Save and checking 'Save AutoRecover information'.

Exporting for Broader Use

Once securely saved, you might find a need to export your data to different formats for various uses. Excel's exporting capabilities allow you to convert your workbooks into formats like PDF or XPS, catering to needs ranging from emailing a report to publishing a dataset online.

PDF Export

To export a workbook as a PDF:

1. Go to File > Export > Create PDF/XPS.
2. Choose where to save the file.
3. Decide if you want to export the entire workbook or just the current sheet.
4. Click Publish.

Such a PDF is perfect when you need a format that maintains the layout and formatting, suitable for email attachments or professional printing.

Sharing for Collaboration

The true power of digital tools today lies in collaboration. Excel supports multiple ways to share your workbooks, ensuring that teamwork on data analysis and decision-making is seamless and efficient.

Excel Online: Real-Time Collaboration

If you use Excel as part of Microsoft 365, you have access to Excel Online, which allows multiple users to work on the same document in real-time. This is ideal for collaborative projects where team members need to input data or review findings simultaneously.

To share a workbook:

1. Click on File > Share > Save to Cloud, then choose a location in OneDrive or SharePoint.
2. Once saved, click on the 'Share' button, enter the email addresses of your collaborators, and set the permissions (Can Edit or Can View).
3. Send the invite. Recipients will be able to access and work on the workbook in real-time, directly from their browsers.

Permissions and Security

When sharing any document, it's crucial to manage who has access and to what extent. Excel allows you to set permissions that can limit users' abilities to edit, copy, or even print documents. This ensures that sensitive information does not go beyond intended viewership.

To set permissions:

1. Go to File > Info > Protect Workbook.
2. Choose from options like 'Encrypt with Password', 'Restrict Access', or 'Add a Digital Signature'.

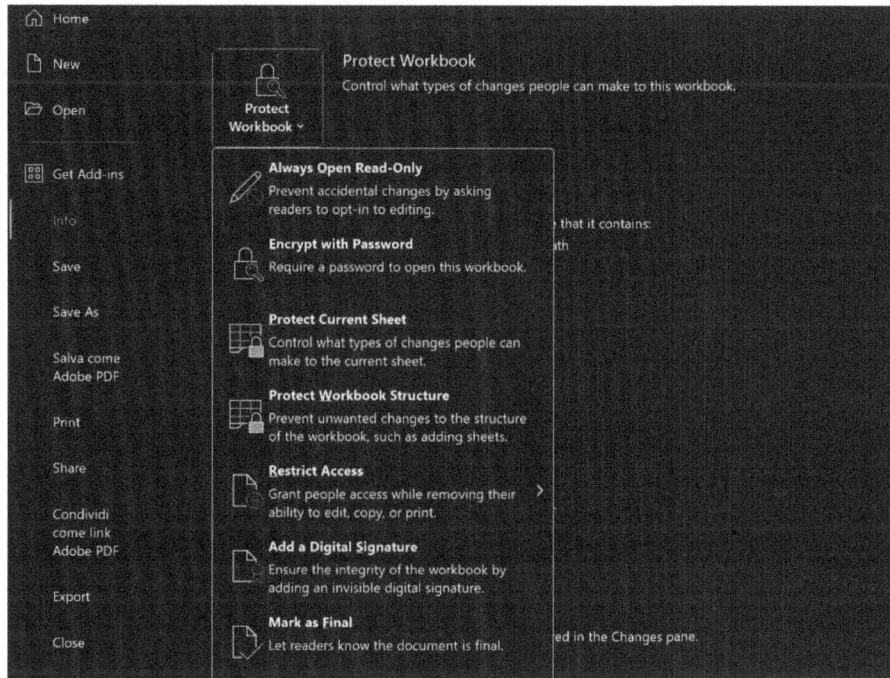

This ensures your data is shared securely, minimizing the risk of unauthorized access.

By mastering these methods of saving, exporting, and sharing your workbooks, you turn routine tasks into strategic processes that safeguard your data, ensure its flexible use across platforms, and empower collaborative workflows. Remember, proper management of these functions is foundational not just to the security of your data but to the efficiency and effectiveness of your overall workflow in Excel. As we move forward in our journey, reinforced by this knowledge, think about these functionalities as tools in your arsenal, ready to deploy as you transform raw data into impactful business insights.

CHAPTER 2: WORKING WITH DATA AND FORMATTING

Delving into Excel might seem daunting at first, but once you've stepped past the initial acquaintance, it's time to start interacting more intricately with this powerful tool. In the world of Excel, data isn't just numbers and text; it's the very backbone of informed decision-making and efficient work processes. This chapter is all about mastering the art of working with data and formatting it to your will—skills that are fundamental for anyone looking to excel in, well, Excel.

Imagine you've just been handed a raw gem. It's valuable, sure, but not nearly as much as it could be. The same goes for raw data in Excel. Without proper formatting and management, data remains in a state of potential. Our goal is to transform this raw potential into a polished gem—making your data not only presentable but powerfully functional.

First, we tackle data entry. It's not just about typing numbers or text into cells. It's about doing it smartly. Features like AutoFill and Flash Fill aren't just tools; they are your companions that save hours of manual input, learning your patterns, and assisting along the way. Then there's the art of data types. Excel is not a one-size-fits-all environment; understanding the specific nature of the data you're working with can dramatically increase both accuracy and efficiency.

Next, we move on to formatting. This isn't just about making your spreadsheet pretty. It's about clarity and usability. Proper cell formatting turns a spreadsheet from a mere table into a clear, readable, and persuasive document. Whether you're conditioning cell formats based on the data they hold, or highlighting key insights with Conditional Formatting, these skills ensure that your data tells a story, clearly and compellingly.

And while the precise arrangement of windows might seem a marginal skill, mastering how to freeze panes or split your workspace effectively can mean the difference between an easy task and a logistical headache, especially when dealing with large datasets.

By the end of this chapter, handling data in Excel will feel less like a chore and more like a craft—where every cell you format right, every piece of data correctly entered, adds up to a masterpiece of efficiency and clarity. Let's dive in and turn that potential into prowess.

DATA ENTRY BEST PRACTICES (AUTOFILL, FLASH FILL, DATA TYPES)

In the realm of Excel, efficiency isn't just an option; it's a necessity. Particularly when it comes to data entry, leveraging Excel's in-built features not only accelerates the process but also minimizes the potential for errors, ensuring that the data you input lays a solid foundation for whatever analyses or tasks you plan to perform later. So, let's dive deep into the world of Excel and explore best practices for data entry, focusing keenly on AutoFill, Flash Fill, and understanding data types.

AutoFill: Your First Step to Smarter Work

Think of AutoFill as your diligent assistant, ready to take over repetitive tasks with precision. This feature isn't just about saving time; it's about maintaining consistency across your data set. Here's how you can make the most out of AutoFill:

1. **Basic Sequences**: Start with something simple. Enter a number or a date in a cell, select the cell, then hover over the bottom right corner until you see a tiny cross. Drag down or across and watch as Excel fills in the subsequent numbers or dates for you. This works for days, months, years, or even pre-defined lists like January to December.

2. **Complex Patterns**: Excel's intelligence extends beyond simple sequences. If you start with an increment pattern (say, 2, 4, 6), AutoFill will pick it up and continue it. This method works beautifully for financial projections, time series analysis, or any scenario where data follows a predictable pattern.

3. **Custom Lists**: You might not know this, but Excel allows you to create custom AutoFill lists. If your work requires frequently entering specific sequences (product codes, department names, geographic locations), setting up a custom list can be a game-changer, turning a morning's work into a minute's task.

Embracing Flash Fill: The Intuitive Typist

Where AutoFill handles well-defined patterns, Flash Fill excels in understanding and executing more complex and nuanced data entries. If you're working with data that follows a certain artistic but consistent style, Flash Fill is your go-to tool.

1. **Splitting Data**: Imagine you have a list of full names, and you need to split them into first names and last names in different columns. Simply type the first name from the first cell into a new adjacent cell. Start typing the second, and watch Excel intuit what you're doing, offering to complete the list for you via Flash Fill.

2. **Combining Data**: The reverse is also seamless with Flash Fill. If you have first names in one column and last names in another, typing a full name in a new column triggers Excel to offer filling the rest based on your pattern.

3. **Formatting Adjustments**: Flash Fill can recognize patterns in data formatting as well. This could mean transforming dates, abbreviations, or even capitalization styles across multiple entries without breaking a sweat.

Understanding and Utilizing Data Types

Data types in Excel are crucial because they tell Excel how to treat the data inside each cell. This could be as simple as distinguishing text from numbers, or as complex as handling financial or date information.

1. **Text vs. Numbers**: Excel differentiates between text data and numerical data, a distinction that affects how it processes formulas and functions applied to that data. Knowing when data should be input as text (like phone numbers or postal codes) or numbers is crucial.

2. **Using Special Data Types**: Excel has evolved to handle more than just text and numbers. With special data types like Stocks or Geography, you can pull in rich, linked data right into your worksheet. For instance, typing in a country name and setting it as a 'Geography' data type allows Excel to fill related information, like population or capital, which you can then reference dynamically in your work.

Putting It All Together: A Practical Scenario

Imagine you're tasked with creating an employee database. You need to record names, start dates, and some financial data across several years. Utilizing AutoFill, you can quickly fill out the dates of employment. With Flash Fill, split names entered in a single column into first and last names in separate columns seamlessly. Finally, by setting the appropriate data types for salary figures, you ensure that Excel can automatically undertake numerical calculations including summing totals or calculating tax deductions without you needing to continually adjust formatting or rectify data handling errors.

This step-by-step approach not only reduces the hours of work typically associated with data entry but also ensures that your data is clean, organized, and ready for any analytical task you might need to perform. Remember, the key to Excel proficiency lies in harnessing these features to work smarter, not harder. This will set the foundation for further exploration and more advanced operations in this versatile tool. As we progress through this guide, each tool and technique will build upon what we've established here, rounding out a comprehensive mastery of Excel designed for real-world application.

CELL FORMATTING: NUMBER, TEXT, AND CUSTOM FORMATS

When you start to imagine Excel as not just a data entry tool but as a canvas for presenting information, the importance of cell formatting leaps to the forefront. Whether you are preparing a report for the board, analyzing financial statements, or organizing a list of upcoming events, how information is formatted in Excel can drastically impact readability and interpretation. Let's navigate through the essentials of cell formatting, exploring number, text, and custom formats, and unravel how you can tailor these to fit your precise needs.

The Significance of Number Formats

Excel is adept at handling numbers because at its core, it is designed to process, analyze, and display numerical data efficiently. Numerical formats in Excel encompass a wide array of specificities, from currency and percentages to date-time formats and fractions. Grasping how to apply these appropriately is pivotal.

1. **General Format**: The default setting in Excel does not add any formatting. It displays numbers just as you type them. It's straightforward but remember, using a more specific format can often be more useful for clear data interpretation.

2. **Currency and Accounting**: These are vital for financial documents. Currency format adds the currency symbol right next to the number, which is ideal for pricing lists, while the Accounting format aligns the dollar signs at the edge of the cell, which enhances readability in financial statements.

3. **Percentage Format**: When dealing with ratios or statistics, converting a decimal to a percentage can make your data more intuitive. To apply it, simply select your cells and click the Percent Style button in the Home toolbar. This converts existing decimals into percentages, aiding in clearer, instant comprehension.

4. **Date and Time**: Proper representation of dates and times is crucial for keeping track of chronological data. Excel offers a variety of date and time formats and understanding how to apply these can help in maintaining clear records of events, schedules, and deadlines.

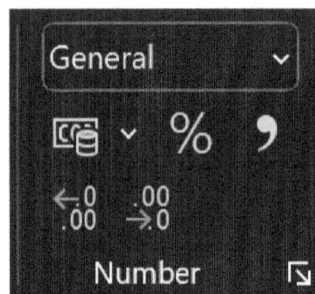

Mastering Text Formats

While numbers are integral to Excel, text formatting plays a crucial role, especially when your data includes a significant amount of textual information. Proper text formatting ensures that such information is as impactful and clear as your numerical data.

1. **Wrap Text**: Often, you'll encounter cell content that surpasses the default column width. By enabling 'Wrap Text', Excel adjusts the row height, allowing the cell's content to be displayed across multiple lines within the same cell. This is particularly useful for lengthy headers or descriptions.

2. **Merge and Center**: For titles or headings spanning multiple columns, 'Merge and Center' combines selected cells into one and centers the text within. This not only tidies up the appearance but also makes headings distinct and noticeable.

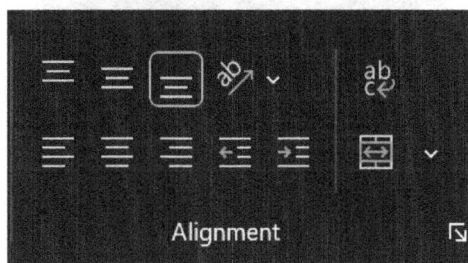

Customizing Your Data with Custom Formats

Sometimes pre-defined formats don't exactly meet your needs. That's where custom formats come into play. Excel's custom formatting provides a flexible tool to precisely define how your numbers, text, and dates are displayed.

1. **Creating Conditional Formats**: Let's say you want negative numbers to appear in red and positive in green. Excel allows you to set these conditions easily within the Format Cells dialog. This not only makes your spreadsheet visually intuitive but also aids quickly in identifying trends and outliers.

2. **Using Custom Codes**: For number formats, you can control the display of decimals, how zeros are shown, and even insert textual elements. For example, if you need to display numbers as part of inventory IDs or employee numbers, custom formats can include text elements and numbers together, like ID001, ID002, etc.

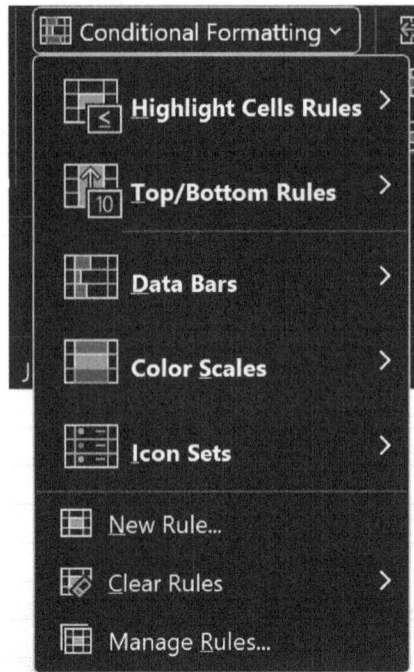

Practical Scenario: Enhancing a Sales Report

Imagine you are creating a monthly sales report. Here's how effective formatting can transform your spreadsheet:

- **Use currency formats** for sales figures to provide immediate financial context.
- **Apply date formats** to sales dates to ensure consistency and ease of understanding.
- **Utilize text wrapping** in the product description cells so each product's full name is visible without expanding columns.
- **Employ conditional formatting** for sales figures to highlight exceptional performances and areas needing attention.

By adjusting each of these aspects, your sales report not only becomes more functional but also more professional-looking and easier to analyze. Each cell's format contributes to a clearer, more immediate understanding of the data, ensuring that the report effectively communicates the intended information.

Through precise and thoughtful application of formatting tools in Excel, mundane data can be transformed into a well-organized, visually appealing, and insightful document. Whether it's through basic application of number formats, leveraging text formatting to improve readability, or deploying custom formats to meet specific presentation requirements, mastering cell formatting is a critical skill on your journey to becoming proficient in Excel. This foundational knowledge empowers you to manipulate data presentation efficiently and tailor your spreadsheets to not only meet but exceed the demands of your professional environment.

CONDITIONAL FORMATTING: HIGHLIGHTING KEY INSIGHTS

Embarking on a journey into the depths of Excel brings us to one of its most visually impactful tools: Conditional Formatting. It's a feature that can transform the way you view and organize your data. Through Conditional Formatting, Excel allows you to apply specific formatting to cells that meet certain criteria. This isn't just about making your spreadsheet look good—it's about instantly highlighting the critical insights your data offers, which is essential in making informed decisions quickly.

The Power of Visual Cues

Let's start with why Conditional Formatting is so powerful. By using visual cues such as colors, icons, and data bars, this tool helps you quickly spot trends, identify exceptions, and categorize data efficiently. For instance, you might use a color scale to show lower and higher values in different shades, or apply an icon set that visually ranks data from highest to lowest based on specific thresholds.

Setting Up Basic Conditional Formats

Imagine you have a sales report with monthly figures. You want to quickly ascertain which months exceeded targets and which fell short. Here's how you could set up Conditional Formatting to achieve this:

1. **Highlight Above or Below Average**: You select the sales data and choose to highlight cells that are above average. Excel automatically shades these cells, say in green, allowing you to instantly see which months performed better than average. Conversely, you could highlight below-average months in red to draw attention to periods of underperformance.
2. **Data Bars**: These add a visual bar within your cell, proportional to the cell's value relative to the rest of the selected range. Applying this to your sales data could help you visualize the volume of sales each month at a glance, without needing to digest the specific numbers.

Utilizing Formulas in Conditional Formatting

Conditional Formatting isn't limited to straightforward numeric thresholds. By incorporating formulas, you can customize this tool to fit more complex analytical needs. Suppose you're tracking project deadlines and want to highlight dates that are approaching within the next week:

1. **Using Formulas for Dates**: You might use a formula within Conditional Formatting to check if the date in a cell is within the next seven days.

Excel could then highlight these upcoming deadlines in yellow, helping you manage your priorities without manually searching through dates.

Advanced Techniques: Beyond Basic Highlights

As you become more comfortable with basic Conditional Formatting, you might explore some advanced techniques that can offer deeper insights:

1. **Top/Bottom Rules**: This is perfect for quickly identifying outliers or key performers. For example, in a dataset of test scores, highlighting the top 10% can immediately point out the high achievers.
2. **Using Color Scales Wisely**: Applying a color gradient can help in understanding data distribution at a glance. For temperature data, a gradient from blue (cool) to red (hot) can make daily readings much more intuitive.
3. **Custom Icon Sets**: These allow you to set specific icons for different data ranges. In a financial overview, you might set a "dollar" icon for profitable departments and a "warning" icon for ones that are not meeting financial expectations.

Real-World Application: Monitoring Employee Performance

Let's consider a practical scenario where you're tasked with monitoring employee performance metrics. You could set up Conditional Formatting to reflect various performance levels:

- **Green** for performance metrics that are on target.
- **Orange** for metrics that are near target but require attention.
- **Red** for metrics that are significantly below target.

Such visual differentiation allows managers to quickly digest the performance landscape and intervene where necessary, without getting bogged down by numbers.

Integration with Business Intelligence

In a business environment, Conditional Formatting can play a pivotal role in dashboard and report design, enhancing readability and providing immediate visual context. It's especially useful in dynamic reports where data updates regularly and maintaining oversight is key.

The Art of Refinement

As with any powerful tool, the key to using Conditional Formatting effectively lies in its thoughtful application. Overuse can make a spreadsheet crowded and confusing. The aim should always be to enhance clarity—not create noise. By judiciously using Conditional Formatting, you keep your data interaction both efficient and insightful.

Through careful application and a bit of creativity, Conditional Formatting becomes not just a function of Excel but a robust analytical tool that makes your data speak vividly. This capability to convey complex data points effectively through visual cues is invaluable, whether you're making high-stakes business decisions, managing everyday tasks, or simply trying to understand your data better. In the coming chapters, as we explore more complex functionalities, remember that these foundational tools like Conditional Formatting are stepping stones to advanced data manipulation and presentation in Excel.

FREEZING PANES, SPLITTING WINDOWS, AND DATA ORGANIZATION

In the world of data analysis and spreadsheet management, navigating through extensive datasets can be quite the odyssey. We've all been there—you scroll down through rows of data, and suddenly, your headers disappear into the abyss above. Or perhaps, you're comparing figures across a vast horizontal dataset and lose track of your columns. This is where mastering the art of pane freezing and window splitting becomes essential, not just for ease but for efficiency in working with large datasets in Excel.

The Magic of Freezing Panes

Freezing panes in Excel allows you to keep row and column labels visible as you scroll through your data. It's incredibly helpful when dealing with extensive datasets where losing sight of headers can lead to confusion and errors.

Imagine you are analyzing a yearly financial report with data for each month listed horizontally. The column headers signify each month, and as you scroll right to view December's data, January's figures scroll out of view. By freezing the top row or the first few columns, you ensure that no matter how far you scroll, your reference points remain constant.

How it works: You can freeze panes easily via the View tab on the Excel ribbon. You decide whether to freeze the top row, the first column, or freeze several rows and columns based on your current cell selection. The process is intuitive—select the row below or the column to the right of where you want the split, and then apply the freeze.

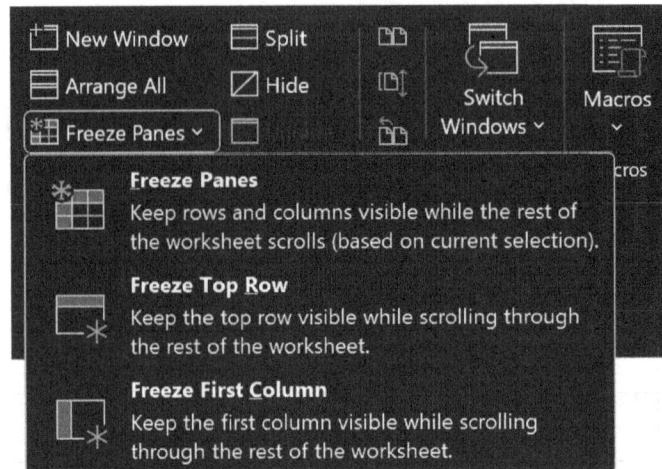

Splitting Windows for Comparative Tasks

Splitting windows is another invaluable technique for managing large datasets. While freezing panes keeps parts of your sheet static, splitting actually divides your Excel window into two or four independent panes that can scroll separately. This is particularly useful when you want to compare data from different sections of your worksheet without continuously scrolling back and forth. Consider you're managing a staff roster and simultaneously monitoring attendance records which are spaced far apart on the same sheet. By splitting the window, you can view and operate on both sections simultaneously, making it far easier to cross-reference or update information on the fly.

Application: Splitting is easily activated by dragging the split bars located above the vertical and horizontal scroll bars, or by using the Split option in the View tab. You can adjust how much of the sheet each pane occupies, tailoring it to the specific needs of your workflow.

Effective Data Organization Strategies

Understanding the layout strategies in large Excel files goes beyond freezing and splitting. Effective organization involves a clear strategy for how data is arranged—this can mean the difference between a user-friendly spreadsheet and a confusing one.

1. **Tables**: Converting a range of data into a formatted table (using the 'Format as Table' feature) not only improves the visual appeal but introduces powerful data management tools such as sorting, filtering, and automatic filling of formulas. Tables support structured references, where formulas adjust automatically as you add rows or columns.

2. **Layering Information**: Avoid the temptation to cram too much information into a single worksheet. Using multiple sheets within a workbook can help you organize data logically.

For example, keeping raw data on one sheet, analytical summaries on another, and graphical representations on yet another can make navigation and comprehension more manageable.

3. **Data Validation**: This is crucial for maintaining data integrity, especially in large datasets where manual errors are likely. Data validation rules in Excel can restrict what data can fit into a cell range—whether it's preventing illogical dates or ensuring that only predetermined categories can be entered.

Practical Scenario: Handling Sales Data

Let's apply these techniques to a practical scenario: managing annual sales data for multiple product lines across various regions. Each product and region has its own monthly sales figures, and quarterly summaries.

- **Freeze Panes**: Freeze the top row containing your month labels and the first column containing your product names so these labels remain visible as you scroll to view different parts of the data.

- **Split Windows**: If your worksheet extends to both a large number of rows and columns, use splitting to compare the early months' data directly against later months without losing sight of either.

- **Use Tables**: Convert your data range into a table for cleaner management and to utilize powerful built-in features that facilitate data handling.

By integrating these methods, navigating your sales report becomes less of a challenge and more of a strategic exploration, revealing insights with ease and precision. This doesn't just save time—it ensures that the data you work so hard to analyze delivers its full potential in guiding business decisions.

These techniques, while simple on the surface, are fundamental to mastering Excel's environment. Whether you're preparing financial reports, managing inventory, or tracking project timelines, being proficient in these areas of Excel ensures you're not just working hard but working smart.

CHAPTER 3: INTRODUCTION TO FUNCTIONS AND FORMULAS

Welcome to the core of Excel where magic begins to happen right at your fingertips—functions and formulas. Imagine you're a chef in a well-equipped kitchen. Until now, you've been familiarizing yourself with tools and ingredients—where they're located and how to neatly arrange them. Now, it's time to start mixing these ingredients to create something extraordinary. In Excel, our ingredients are the data and our recipes are the functions and formulas.

Let me tell you a story of Sam, a finance manager, whose days were swamped with data entry and manually calculating revenue projections. His turning point came when he harnessed the power of simple Excel functions. By using just SUM and AVERAGE, he cut his weekly data-crunching time by half. This not only boosted his productivity but also allowed him more time to strategize and focus on higher-level tasks.

Functions and formulas are Excel's way of simplifying your calculations and data analysis. They can sum up sales in seconds, calculate averages, or even sort through and organize your data with logical functions. The beauty lies in their ability to automate repetitive tasks, minimize human error, and importantly, save an incredible amount of time—something all of us surely appreciate. This isn't about memorizing every function or mastering complex formulas overnight. It's about understanding the structure of how formulas work and identifying which function to use and when. Consider this chapter your gateway to turning raw data into meaningful insights with a few keystrokes.

By the end of our journey today, you'll not only know the basics like SUM and AVERAGE but also navigate through more intricate paths using IF and VLOOKUP. Each formula you learn will build your confidence and gradually unveil the broader landscape of possibilities within Excel, much like Sam, who transitioned from a task-oriented manager to a strategic asset in his company.

So, let's roll up our sleeves and start cooking some delicious Excel recipes that will surely spice up your data management skills and accelerate your professional journey.

UNDERSTANDING FORMULA STRUCTURE AND CELL REFERENCES ($, RELATIVE, ABSOLUTE)

Understanding the structure of Excel formulas and the types of cell references—absolute, relative, and mixed—is somewhat akin to learning the rules of a new language. It may seem daunting at first, but once you grasp these concepts, a world of efficiency and accuracy opens up in your data management tasks.

Let's begin with the basics of a formula. At its heart, a formula in Excel is an expression used to calculate and process data.

It always starts with an equal sign (=), which signals Excel that what follows is a calculation. After the equal sign, you include the elements you want to calculate. These can be numbers, cell references, functions, or a mix of all three.

Relative References

Imagine telling someone to always take a seat one row up and one seat to the right from where they currently are in an auditorium. No matter where they start, they move in the same relative pattern—up one, right one. In Excel, relative references work the same way.

When you use a relative reference in a formula, you're telling Excel to use a cell's position relative to the position of the cell containing the formula. This means if you copy or move the formula across your workbook, the references will adjust automatically.

For instance, say you have a formula in cell C1 that reads =A1+B1. If you copy this formula down to C2, it automatically changes to =A2+B2. Each cell adjusts according to its new position, making relative references particularly useful for applying the same operation across multiple rows or columns.

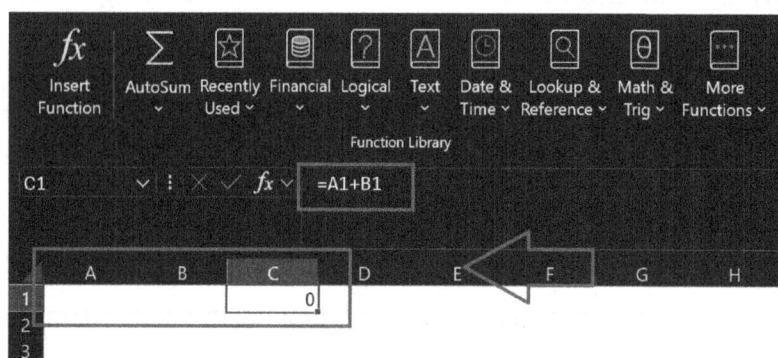

Absolute References

Now, let's change the scenario. Suppose you are instructing someone to always sit in seat B3, no matter where they start from in the auditorium. This fixed reference point is akin to using absolute references in Excel.

In Excel formulas, you make a cell reference absolute by placing a dollar sign ($) before the column letter and/or row number. For example, A1 means that no matter where you copy your formula, it will always refer to cell A1.

Why is this useful? Imagine you have a workbook where you need to multiply several numbers by a constant value, say a tax rate located in cell A2. By setting A2 as an absolute reference (=A2), you can copy the formula across the workbook, and it will always calculate using the tax rate from A2, ensuring consistency and avoiding manual errors.

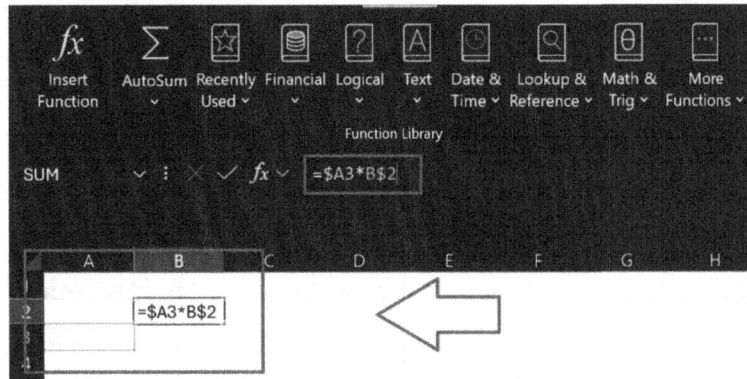

Mixed References

Sometimes, you might need a hybrid approach. This is where mixed references come into play. In mixed references, you can fix either the row or the column. For example, $A1 locks the reference to column A but allows the row number to adjust. Conversely, A$1 locks the reference to row 1 while permitting the column to change.

This flexibility can be particularly advantageous in situations where you want to maintain a constant reference either across rows or down columns. Suppose you're calculating the costs for various items across multiple regions. You might fix the row that contains prices while allowing columns (representing different regions) to vary.

Practical Application

Let's concrete these ideas with a real-world application to ensure they are not just theoretical concepts. Consider a sales report where you are tasked with calculating the total sales for multiple products across different regions. Your worksheet includes prices in one column (column B), units sold in the adjacent column (column C), and you want to calculate total sales in column D.

1. In cell D1, you'd start with a simple multiplication formula =B1*C1. Dragging this down the column, Excel uses relative references to adjust each formula to its rows—B2*C2, B3*C3, and so on.

2. Suppose you also need to apply a discount stored in cell F1. If you want to include this in your calculation, your formula in D1 changes to =B1*C1*F1. Copying this formula down the column keeps the reference to the discount rate constant, thanks to the absolute reference to F1, while still adjusting the product price and units sold per row.

Understanding how to effectively use different types of cell references will not only safeguard against common errors but also enhance your ability to manage large datasets efficiently.

As you become more familiar with when to use each type of reference, you'll find that you're able to streamline your workflow significantly, allowing you more time to analyze the results rather than just compiling them.

Excel, with its robust set of tools for data manipulation, relies heavily on these foundational concepts of cell references. Mastering them enables you to harness the full potential of this powerful software, turning what can be overwhelming data sets into manageable and insightful information.

BASIC FORMULAS: SUM, AVERAGE, MIN, MAX, COUNT

When you start working with Excel, some of the first tools in your arsenal are the basic arithmetic and counting functions. These functions are the bread and butter of Excel users across all sectors—from education and finance to healthcare and beyond. They're fundamental not only because they're simple, but because they perform essential calculations that serve as building blocks for more complex tasks.

The SUM Function

The SUM function is probably one of the most used functions in Excel. It does exactly what it sounds like—it sums up numbers. Let's say you own a bookstore and you want to find out your total sales for the week from different genres. Each genre—romance, science fiction, mystery, and non-fiction—is represented in columns from B to E. The SUM function allows you to quickly calculate the total sales across all these genres.

Imagine you put the daily sales figures in cells B2 through E2 for Monday, B3 through E3 for Tuesday, and so forth till Friday. To get the total weekly sales for all genres, in cell F2, you would write:

$$=SUM(B2:E2)$$

This formula tells Excel to sum the values across cells B2 to E2. You can drag this formula down from F2 to F6 to replicate this calculation for the entire week.

The AVERAGE Function

Now, knowing your total sales is useful, but what if you need to calculate the average daily sales per genre to understand which genre sells best consistently? The AVERAGE function comes in handy here. It computes the mean or average of numbers in a range of cells.

Using the same bookstore example, if you wanted to calculate the average sales from Monday to Friday for the romance genre (let's assume these figures are in column B from B2 to B6), you would enter in cell B7:

$$=AVERAGE(B2:B6)$$

This function tells Excel to find the average sales from cells B2 to B6, giving you a clearer picture of how romance books performed across the week.

The MIN and MAX Functions

Sometimes, extremes can be more telling than averages. The MIN and MAX functions find the smallest and largest values in a range, respectively. These functions are particularly useful in scenarios where you need to identify outliers or extremes.

Suppose in your bookstore, you're also tracking the daily number of visitors. If you have this data from Monday to Friday in cells G2 to G6, and you want to know the day with the least and most foot traffic, you would use:

$$=MIN(G2:G6)$$

for the day with the lowest foot traffic, and

$$=MAX(G2:G6)$$

for the day with the highest foot traffic.

These functions quickly highlight days that might require further analysis for unusually low or high visitor counts.

The COUNT Function

Lastly, the COUNT function is essential for getting quick insights into your data sets. It counts the number of cells in a range that contain numbers. This function is incredibly useful when you want to know how many entries or data points you have without manually counting each one.

If you're using an additional column in your bookstore spreadsheet to track the number of promotional materials given out each day, and not every day this activity is performed, the COUNT function can tell you on how many days the promotional materials were distributed. Assuming this data is in column H from H2 to H6, in cell H7 you could input:

$$=COUNT(H2:H6)$$

This would give you the number of days promotional materials were handed out, helping you measure the outreach effort.

Practical Applications and Tips

These basic functions, while simple, can be incredibly powerful in analyzing and understanding your data. Tips for using them more effectively include:

- **Check your data range correctly:** Always ensure that the correct cells are included in your function to avoid errors in calculation.
- **Combine functions for more powerful insights:** You can combine these basic functions with other Excel tools like conditional formatting to highlight when certain thresholds are reached (e.g., when daily sales exceed a set target).
- **Use absolute and relative references wisely:** When copying formulas that use these basic functions, keep in mind whether your cell references should adjust automatically (relative) or remain constant (absolute).

Understanding and implementing these basic functions effectively sets the stage for mastering more intricate tasks in Excel. These functions not only help you perform everyday calculations with ease but also build a foundation for tackling more complex analytical tasks efficiently. Whether managing a bookstore, overseeing a hospital's patient records, or analyzing financial reports, mastering these fundamental Excel tools empowers you to handle data with confidence and precision.

LOGICAL FUNCTIONS: IF, AND, OR, IFERROR

In the realm of Excel, logical functions are like the decision-makers in your sheets, guiding actions based on specific conditions. These functions are critical for performing intelligent data analyses and automations, allowing you to manage information dynamically and with significant nuance. Let's delve into some of the most commonly used logical functions: IF, AND, OR, and IFERROR.

The IF Function

At its core, the IF function is Excel's basic decision-making tool. It checks whether a condition is met, and returns one value if true, and another if false. Think of it as a digital crossroads where Excel decides which path to take based on the information you provide.

For instance, suppose you manage an employee database and need to determine eligibility for a year-end bonus. Employees with more than $50,000 in sales qualify for the bonus. In your Excel sheet, if column A lists employee names and column B their annual sales, you might place the following formula in column C:

=IF(B2>50000, "Eligible", "Not Eligible")

This formula instructs Excel to check if the sales figure in cell B2 is greater than 50,000. If true, Excel displays "Eligible" in cell C2. If false, it shows "Not Eligible." By copying this formula down the column, you can quickly determine the bonus eligibility for your entire list.

The AND Function

When you need Excel to consider multiple conditions before making a decision, the AND function is your go-to tool. It returns TRUE if all the conditions are met, otherwise FALSE. This function is especially useful when filtering data based on several criteria needs to be met simultaneously. Consider a scenario where you're administering a scholarship. Applicants must be both a junior or senior and must have a GPA of 3.5 or higher. Assuming "Year" is in column D and "GPA" is in column E, your formula might look like this:

=AND(D2="Senior", E2>=3.5)

This formula checks that both conditions (being a senior and having a GPA of 3.5 or higher) are satisfied. It's a straightforward, powerful way to sift through data.

The OR Function

Contrary to AND, the OR function is less strict; it requires only one of the conditions to be true. This function is perfect for tasks where multiple criteria can individually qualify a data point. Imagine you're organizing a special event for clients who either placed orders over $1000 last year or have been active clients for over 5 years. Assuming "Last Year's Order" is in column F and "Years as Client" is in column G, your invite list criteria in Excel would be defined as:

=OR(F2>1000, G2>=5)

This setup allows Excel to return TRUE and thus select a client if they meet either of the specified conditions.

The IFERROR Function

In data processing, encountering errors is common, particularly when formulas depend on other cells that might contain errors or are empty. The IFERROR function improves the resilience of your worksheets by catching these errors and replacing them with a custom message or alternative calculation.

Suppose you're calculating the division of sales by the number of transactions, but some transactions might be recorded as zero, leading to division errors. If "Total Sales" are in column H and "Number of Transactions" in column I, you could use IFERROR to handle possible division errors:

$$=IFERROR(H2/I2, "Check Data")$$

This formula attempts the division; if an error occurs (like division by zero), it displays "Check Data" instead of the default error message, thus maintaining the cleanliness and usefulness of your data report.

Harnessing Logical Functions in Real-world Applications

The power of logical functions becomes evident when dealing with large datasets that require decision-making based on multiple criteria. By incorporating these functions into your Excel toolkit, you can automate these decisions, saving time and reducing the potential for human error. Here are some practical tips for using logical functions effectively:

- **Be clear about your conditions:** Logical functions depend heavily on the accuracy of the conditions you define. Ensure your criteria are precise and reflect the necessary requirements.
- **Combine functions for more complexity:** Don't hesitate to nest one function inside another to handle complex scenarios. For example, an IF function can be used inside an AND function to create more layered decision-making logic.

Logical functions bring structure and automation to your Excel spreadsheets. They not only make your sheets "smarter" but also streamline your workflow, allowing you to focus more on analysis and less on mundane data processing. Understanding and applying these functions will undoubtedly elevate your Excel proficiency and enable you to manage data more effectively in any professional setting.

DATE & TIME FUNCTIONS: TODAY, NOW, YEAR, NETWORKDAYS

In Excel, managing dates and times is not merely about entering values into cells. These data types are pivotal for scheduling, analyzing trends, and performing time-sensitive calculations. Let's explore some of Excel's fundamental date and time functions: TODAY, NOW, YEAR, and NETWORKDAYS. Each serves a unique purpose in streamlining operations and enhancing your data management capabilities.

The TODAY Function

Imagine you are a project manager and need to constantly update project statuses based on the current date. Manually entering today's date repeatedly can be cumbersome and error-prone. This is where the TODAY function becomes invaluable. The function does not require any arguments and automatically populates the current date.

For instance, to check if a project deadline has passed, you might compare the deadline date in cell A2 with today's date:

$$=TODAY()>A2$$

If the result is TRUE, it indicates the deadline has passed. Embedding the TODAY function in your spreadsheets ensures that any date comparison remains dynamic and automatically updates each day without manual intervention.

The NOW Function

While TODAY is useful for date-specific tasks, the NOW function takes it a step further by including the current time. This function is particularly useful in environments where time down to the minute is critical, such as logging exact entry times in a time tracking spreadsheet.

Consider you are logging issues in a customer support center and need to record the exact time a complaint was registered. In cell B2, you could use:

$$=NOW()$$

This formula inserts the current date and time, providing a precise timestamp of when the complaint was logged. Like TODAY, NOW updates itself every time the spreadsheet is recalculated, ensuring all time records are up-to-date.

The YEAR Function

Often, data sets include full dates, but sometimes you need just the year component for annual reports or trend analysis. This is where the YEAR function becomes essential. It extracts the year from a given date, allowing for simplified year-on-year comparisons and summarizations.

Suppose your company's sales data from the past five years are in column A. To analyze annual sales, you might first need to extract the year from each date:

$$=YEAR(A2)$$

By applying this function down the column, you can quickly categorize sales data by year, making it easier to compare how your business has performed over the years.

The NETWORKDAYS Function

Project management often requires an understanding of working days between two dates—for instance, calculating the number of workdays required to complete a task. The NETWORKDAYS function calculates the number of weekdays between two dates, automatically excluding weekends and optionally a list of specified holidays.

If you need to calculate the working days between a project start date in cell A2 and an end date in B2, your formula would look like this:

=NETWORKDAYS(A2, B2)

Additionally, if you want to exclude holidays that impact work progress, you can list them in a range, say D2:D10, and modify your formula:

=NETWORKDAYS(A2, B2, D2:D10)

This adjustment ensures that your workday calculation is accurate and reflects the actual number of days workers are available.

Practical Applications and Tips

Utilizing these functions helps automate and accurately perform date and time calculations, essential for efficient project management, trend analysis, and operational planning. Here are some tips for maximizing the efficacy of these functions:

- **Set cell formatting properly:** To ensure that functions like TODAY and NOW display correctly, format the cells to show date and/or time formats as needed.
- **Regularly review and test date-related functions:** Since NOW and TODAY are volatile, meaning they update upon every spreadsheet recalculating, ensure your spreadsheet calculations are operating as intended, especially in complex automations.
- **Use appropriate functions for your needs:** While it might be tempting to overuse NOW for its precision, if only the date is relevant, use TODAY to keep data cleaner and focused.

Harnessing the power of these date and time functions in Excel not only boosts productivity but also brings a high level of precision to your data management tasks. Whether scheduling deadlines, logging real-time data, or conducting annual comparisons, these tools are designed to handle the temporal dimensions of your data efficiently.

CHAPTER 4: ADVANCED EXCEL FUNCTIONS

Welcome to the world where Excel starts feeling like a superpower. By now, you've nailed the basics and dipped your toes into the essentials of functions and formulas. You've started to see how Excel listens, responds, and performs when you input the right commands. Today, we're about to dive deeper into the ocean of possibilities with Excel's advanced functions, and trust me, this is where things begin to get thrilling!

Imagine you're a detective sorting through clues to solve a mystery. Just as a detective uses finer tools to get to the bottom of a case, advanced Excel functions are your high-caliber tools for dissecting complex data. Whether it's shuffling through massive datasets to find meaningful trends or automating repetitive tasks that eat into your productive hours, the functions you are about to learn can transform the way you tackle data.

Have you ever faced the frustration of trying to find specific information in a spreadsheet filled with thousands of rows? You're not alone. Here, the power of functions like VLOOKUP, HLOOKUP, INDEX, and MATCH come into play, acting like your search engines within Excel. They can fetch information in a snap that you might otherwise spend hours trying to locate manually.

Then, there are those times when you're trying to make sense of unstructured data. This is where text functions such as CONCATENATE, TEXTJOIN, and TRIM step up. They help clean and organize your data, making it presentable and easier to analyze. It's like having a personal assistant who preps your data before you dive into the analysis.

Statistical functions—think COUNTIF, AVERAGEIF, RANK—let you perform complex statistical analysis to back your business decisions with solid data evidence. These are your tools for getting not just any answers, but the right ones, guiding you through layers of information to reveal insights that can pivot business strategies and outcomes.

As you learn these functions, envision them as more than formulas. They are your pathway to becoming an Excel wizard, someone who works smarter, not harder, and impresses not just with speed but with striking precision and efficiency. Ready to elevate your Excel game to new heights? Let's go!

LOOKUP FUNCTIONS: VLOOKUP, HLOOKUP, INDEX & MATCH

Embarking on any substantial data analysis, especially within the context of modern-day business or complex research, almost invariably involves an encounter with datasets that are as expansive as they are intricate.

Navigating through these can seem daunting—equivalent to finding a single puzzle piece hidden in multiple rooms. Thankfully, Excel offers some rather exceptional tools for this expedition: the lookup functions.

Mastering VLOOKUP

Let's start with the workhorse of data retrieval in Excel: VLOOKUP. This function is like your go-to detective when you need to find information in a large database, based on a unique identifier. Suppose you're working with a customer database, and you need to find specific customer details based on their unique ID; VLOOKUP helps you do just that.

To perform a basic VLOOKUP, you'll need four pieces of information:

1. **Lookup Value**: This is what you're searching for. In our example, it would be the customer's ID.
2. **Table Array**: The range of columns that contains the data. You must ensure that the lookup value is in the first column of this range.
3. **Column Index Number**: If the table array covers multiple columns, you need to tell Excel which column the data you seek is located in.
4. **Range Lookup**: This is a TRUE or FALSE value where FALSE directs Excel to find an exact match.

Imagine you are tasked with extracting a product price from a list. Your formula in Excel might look something like this:

=VLOOKUP("ProductID123", A2:B100, 2, FALSE)

This formula tells Excel to look for "ProductID123" in the range A2 to B100, and return the value from the second column that corresponds with the row where "ProductID123" is found, ensuring it's an exact match.

HLOOKUP: Horizontal Lookup

While VLOOKUP searches for data vertically in a column, HLOOKUP searches horizontally across a row. This function becomes particularly useful in situations where your data is formatted in rows instead of columns.

For HLOOKUP, the parameters are similar:

- **Lookup Value**: Again, this is what you're searching for, but this time along a row.
- **Table Array**: The range of rows this time, where the first row must include the lookup value.
- **Row Index Number**: Specifies from which row to retrieve the data.

- **Range Lookup**: Used to specify whether to find an exact match.

You may use HLOOKUP in cases where, let's say, yearly data is arranged row-wise and you need the data for a specific year.

INDEX and MATCH: A Powerful Duo

While VLOOKUP and HLOOKUP are profoundly useful, they do have limitations, notably that VLOOKUP cannot look to the left (it always searches the first column of the range and retrieves data to the right). This is where INDEX and MATCH come in—not just as alternatives but as enhancements providing greater flexibility.

INDEX returns the value of a cell within a table based on the row and column number. MATCH, on the other hand, is used to find the position of a lookup value in a row, column, or table. Used together, they can replicate and exceed the functionality of VLOOKUP and HLOOKUP.

The synergy of INDEX and MATCH works as follows:

1. MATCH searches for the lookup value, returning its position within a specified row or column.
2. INDEX uses this position to return the value of a specified cell within a table array.

Here's how you can combine these functions:

=INDEX(B2:B100, MATCH("ProductID123", A2:A100, 0))

In this example, MATCH is searching for "ProductID123" in the range A2:A100 and returns its position. INDEX then uses this position to fetch the corresponding value from the range B2:B100. This combination not only allows for leftward lookups but also provides a significant increase in processing efficiency with very large datasets—something that VLOOKUP could slow down.

Practical Tips and Tricks

- **Always ensure your data range in VLOOKUP does not shift unintentionally**, as VLOOKUP will not auto-adjust the range.
- **Utilize F4 to lock your arrays** in Excel formulas to make your formula consistent across other cells.
- **For large datasets, consider INDEX and MATCH**, as they are generally faster than VLOOKUP or HLOOKUP because they separate the lookup process into two distinct steps.
- **Utilize dropdown lists combined with lookup functions** to create dynamic and user-friendly Excel models. This approach significantly reduces data entry errors and enhances the efficiency of data retrieval.

Incorporating these functions can remarkably transform your data interaction experience. From simplifying search processes to enabling dynamic data retrievals, mastering these might well be your step towards becoming an Excel guru. As you continue your journey, let these tools elevate your analytical capabilities, bringing precision, efficiency, and maybe a bit of magic to your spreadsheets.

TEXT FUNCTIONS: CONCATENATE, TEXTJOIN, TRIM, LEN

Navigating the textual landscape of Excel can often resemble the art of tailoring. Just as a tailor manipulates fabric, cutting and sewing it to suit a particular design, Excel's text functions allow you to manipulate and reshape text data to fit your analytical and presentation needs. Let's explore some of Excel's most useful text functions: CONCATENATE, TEXTJOIN, TRIM, and LEN. These tools are essential for anyone looking to streamline data entry processes, clean data effectively, or create dynamic and informative text-based outputs.

Crafting Cohesion with CONCATENATE

Think of CONCATENATE as the function that brings diverse text strings together. When you have bits of text in various cells that need to be united into a single string, CONCATENATE is your go-to function. For example, imagine you have a spreadsheet with a first name in one column and a last name in another. CONCATENATE helps you easily combine these to display full names in a single cell.

A practical use of CONCATENATE might look something like this:

=CONCATENATE(A2, " ", B2)

This formula takes the first name from cell A2, adds a space (" "), and appends the last name from cell B2, creating a full name in one cell.

Embracing Efficiency with TEXTJOIN

While CONCATENATE is incredibly useful, TEXTJOIN takes text manipulation to the next level. TEXTJOIN offers the additional ability to include a delimiter that you define, which is extremely handy when dealing with lists or creating outputs where consistent separation of text elements is needed.

Let's consider you're tasked with creating a single string from a range of product features listed in separate cells, and you want them separated by commas. TEXTJOIN does this effortlessly:

=TEXTJOIN(", ", TRUE, A2:A10)

Here, ", " acts as a delimiter, TRUE tells Excel to ignore empty cells, and A2:A10 is the range of text to join. This functionality not only saves time but also ensures clarity and consistency in your data presentation.

Streamlining Strings with TRIM

Moving on to the cleaning aspect, TRIM is akin to a polishing tool for your text. It's designed to remove any surplus spaces from text except for single spaces between words. This function is particularly valuable when you import data from other sources, or you're preparing text for uniform database entry.

For instance, if you've got a cell with erratic spacing, TRIM helps streamline it:

$$=TRIM(A2)$$

This formula will clean up the text in cell A2, ensuring that there are no unwanted space characters at the beginning or end of the string, and that all words are separated by a single space.

Measuring Text with LEN

Finally, there's the LEN function, which stands as your measuring tape in the world of text. LEN provides the count of characters in a text string, including spaces. This is useful for adherence to text limits or for validation of data entry.

Suppose you need to ensure that no employee name exceeds 50 characters in a database. LEN can help you quickly identify entries that need to be reviewed:

$$=LEN(A2)$$

This simple formula returns the number of characters in the text located in cell A2, helping you maintain consistency and adhere to required standards.

Practical Tips and Tricks

- **Combine TEXTJOIN and TRIM for cleaner concatenations**. Especially after importing data from other systems or platforms, use TRIM within a TEXTJOIN function to ensure that the concatenated string is neat and free of extra spaces.
- **Use CONCATENATE or TEXTJOIN for dynamic Excel reports**. For instance, when creating headers or descriptions that must include values from your analysis, dynamically link the text to your data calculations.
- **Utilize LEN to enforce data input rules**. When setting up data validation, use LEN to restrict the length of text entries, which is particularly useful in maintaining data integrity and formatting in user-submitted data.

Mastering these functions not only equips you with the means to handle textual information efficiently but also empowers you to maintain cleaner data, produce more readable reports, and ultimately, achieve a greater degree of precision in your work. Text functions, much like the different stitches and cuts in fabric, allow for the creation of tailored, professional, and highly functional data arrangements in Excel. By integrating these tools into your everyday practice, you elevate both the quality and impact of your data management tasks.

STATISTICAL FUNCTIONS: COUNTIF, AVERAGEIF, RANK

In the bustling world of data analysis, Excel's statistical functions like COUNTIF, AVERAGEIF, and RANK serve as indispensable tools. They are the silent assessors in the background, quantifying, summarizing, and ranking data to provide actionable insights. Whether you're monitoring sales performance, evaluating student grades, or analyzing marketing data, these functions handle large datasets with precision and ease, turning raw data into valuable information.

Demystifying COUNTIF

COUNTIF is specially designed for scenarios where you need to count the number of cells that meet a specific criterion within a range. Imagine you're a sales manager needing to quantify how many sales transactions exceeded a certain value, or a teacher looking to count the number of students who scored above a particular grade. COUNTIF simplifies this task.

To employ COUNTIF, you require two parameters:

- **Range**: The range of cells you want to evaluate.

- **Criteria**: The condition that determines which cells to count.

For instance, if you have a list of weekly sales figures in column A and want to find out how many weeks achieved sales over $500, your formula might look like this:

=COUNTIF(A2:A52, ">500")

This formula efficiently tells you how many entries in the range from A2 to A52 exceed 500, simplifying what could otherwise be a tedious manual count.

Streamlining Evaluations with AVERAGEIF

Moving to AVERAGEIF, which extends the functionality of COUNTIF by calculating the average of the numbers in a range that meet a specified criterion. This function is perfect when you need to analyze subgroups within your data.

For a real estate agent, for instance, determining the average price of houses that sold above a specific square footage could lead to insights that refine listing strategies.

AVERAGEIF needs:

- **Range**: The cells to evaluate with the criterion.

- **Criteria**: The condition to meet.

- **Average_range** (optional): The cells to average. If this is omitted, Excel uses the range for both evaluation and averaging.

If a teacher wants to compute the average score of students who passed (assuming a pass is over 50%):

$$=AVERAGEIF(B2:B30, ">50", C2:C30)$$

This formula evaluates scores in B2 to B30, checks which ones are over 50, and then calculates the average of the corresponding cells in C2 to C30.

Ranking with RANK

Lastly, the RANK function allows you to determine the rank of a number in a list of numbers—its size relative to other values. If you're analyzing competitive data, such as sales figures among a sales team or test scores within a school, RANK provides a quick way to understand positions or standings.

Using RANK involves:

- **Number**: The number you want to find the rank for.

- **Ref**: The array or range of data against which the number is ranked.

- **Order** (optional): A number specifying how to rank numbers. Ascending (1) or descending (0).

An example could be finding the rank of a specific salesperson's sales amount within the entire sales team:

$$=RANK(E2, E2:E30, 0)$$

This function ranks the sales amount in E2 against sales amounts in the range E2 to E30 in descending order, helping highlight top performers.

Practical Tips and Tricks

- **Use wildcards with COUNTIF for partial text matches**. If you're working with data where you need to count entries that contain certain text, COUNTIF can accommodate wildcards. For example, =COUNTIF(A2:A100, "*east") counts all cells that end with "east".

- **Combine AVERAGEIF with conditions to streamline data insights**. Narrowing down a dataset to analyze specific subsets provides targeted insights, which can guide more informed decisions.
- **Leverage RANK in dynamic range evaluations** by combining it with other functions like MATCH to adapt the range dynamically to dataset changes, ensuring your rankings are always current despite changes in data length or structure.

By mastering these statistical functions, you're not just crunching numbers—you are unlocking deeper insights into your data, insights that can influence decisions, drive strategies, and ultimately, enhance understanding and performance in various professional and educational settings. As you continue to leverage these tools, remember that each dataset tells a story, and with these functions, you become its keen narrator.

Financial Functions: FV, PMT, NPV, IRR

In the landscape of financial management and investment analysis, Excel emerges as a powerful tool, equipped with functions designed to simplify complex financial calculations. Whether you're planning personal investments, analyzing business project returns, or managing loans and mortgages, understanding how to utilize Excel's financial functions like FV, PMT, NPV, and IRR can significantly enhance your financial decision-making skills. Let's delve into these functions, exploring their practical applications and the wisdom they unlock in financial analysis.

Exploring Future Value with FV

The FV function in Excel is crucial for understanding the future value of an investment, assuming periodic, constant payments and a constant interest rate. This is particularly helpful in scenarios such as saving for retirement or predicting the future value of a trust fund.

The basic components required to work with the FV function include:

- **Rate**: The interest rate per period.
- **Nper**: Total number of payment periods.
- **Pmt**: The payment made each period; it cannot change over the life of the investment.
- **Pv**: The present value, or the total amount that a series of future payments is worth now.
- **Type**: This indicates when payments are due. Set it to 0 if the payment is due at the end of the period, or to 1 if due at the beginning.

Utilizing FV can give you insights into the growth of investments over time under specified conditions, helping in long-term financial planning.

Managing Payments with PMT

The PMT function is about calculating the payment for a loan based on constant payments and a constant interest rate. This is advantageous for anyone looking to establish a budget around loan repayment, whether it's for a home mortgage, a car loan, or business financing.

Simple inputs needed for PMT include:

- **Rate**: Interest rate for each period.

- **Nper**: Number of payments required.

- **Pv**: Present value or principal amount that's borrowed.

Anyone looking to purchase a home could use PMT to determine their monthly mortgage payments, thereby assessing the affordability of the loan offered.

Calculating Net Present Value with NPV

NPV function is a core tool in capital budgeting for evaluating the profitability of an investment or project. It helps in determining the present value of a series of anticipated future cash flows compared to the initial outlay.

To use NPV effectively, you need:

- **Rate**: The discount rate over a single period.

- **Value1, value2…**: List of cash flows corresponding to each period. The first cash flow occurs at the end of the first period.

Business managers frequently use NPV to decide on the profitability of new projects, comparing the present value of all incoming and outgoing cash flows over the life of the project.

Interpreting IRR

The IRR function is pivotal for evaluating the potential profitability of investments. It calculates the internal rate of return for a series of cash flows occurring at regular intervals.

IRR considers:

- **Values**: A series of cash flows that includes the initial investment and net income amounts for each period following it.

Investors use IRR to judge the profitability of potential investments, comparing it to other investment opportunities or a company's hurdle rate to make decisions.

Practical Tips and Tricks

- **Think of FV as a means to forecast financial growth** under hypothetical conditions. It's practical for planning savings or investments.

- **Use PMT to plan finances around liabilities**. It's perfect for understanding how loans can fit into a personal or business budget.

- **Leverage NPV for project evaluation**. It's essential for any business venture involving future investments to use NPV to understand their value in today's dollars.

- **Utilize IRR to prioritize investment opportunities**, allowing a comparison of project returns over time.

Mastering these functions not only equips you with the ability to navigate through the financial aspects of various projects and investments but also empowers you to make informed, data-driven decisions. By integrating the use of FV, PMT, NPV, and IRR into your financial analysis, you bring precision and depth to your assessments, unlocking new opportunities and enhancing financial strategies effectively. Each function offers a key to deeper understanding and better financial governance, making Excel an indispensable part of effective financial planning and analysis.

CHAPTER 5: SORTING, FILTERING, AND DATA VALIDATION

Welcome to Day 3, where we delve into the heart of Excel's powerful data management features. Imagine you're staring at an ocean of data, rows and columns stretching as far as the eye can see. Without the right tools, finding the specific information you need would feel like searching for treasure without a map. Here in Chapter 5, we're going to equip you with that map and more.

Sorting and filtering are your first mates in navigating this vast data sea. Picture this: you have a list of sales from various departments and need to see which items are performing best. With a few clicks, sorting rearranges your data to highlight top sellers, transforming a jumble of numbers into a clear leaderboard. It's like sorting books on a shelf by height or color; suddenly, everything is easier to find.

But what if your needs are more complex? Enter filtering, a tool that lets you hide everything except the information that meets your criteria. Imagine planning a birthday party but only wanting to invite friends who live nearby. Filtering your contact list by location lets you see just those friends, making your planning much smoother.

Now, ensuring your data stays pristine is crucial, which is where data validation comes in. This is like setting rules at the entrance of a club—no sneakers, no jeans, ensuring that only guests in proper attire get through. In Excel terms, it means ensuring that data entered into your spreadsheet follows the rules you've set, like preventing someone from mistakenly entering a date where a dollar amount should be.

By the end of this chapter, not only will you be able to clean up and control your data with more confidence, but you'll also significantly cut down on the time you spend on data management, allowing you to focus more on analysis and decision-making. Whether you're managing a small project or large datasets in a corporate environment, the skills you'll develop today will help you work smarter, not harder. So, let's roll up our sleeves and dive right in!

SORTING DATA: SINGLE AND MULTI-LEVEL SORTING

Imagine you've just received a list of every attendee at an international conference, including details like names, countries, and professions. Now, your task is to organize this list in a way that reveals patterns and insights, perhaps to determine who the most represented professions are or which countries have the highest attendance. This is where your Excel skills on single and multi-level sorting come into play. Let's explore these essential techniques step-by-step, ensuring you can handle data organization challenges smoothly and efficiently.

Single-Level Sorting

Single-level sorting is one of the simplest yet most powerful tools Excel offers for reordering your data. It's particularly useful when you need a quick glance at data in ascending (A to Z, smallest to largest) or descending (Z to A, largest to smallest) order.

Getting Started with Single-Level Sorting

1. **Prepare Your Data**: Ensure your data is well-organized in columns, with each column having a clear header. This facilitates easier identification of the fields you wish to sort by.

2. **Choose Your Sort Column**: Click on any cell in the column by which you want to sort your data. For instance, if you're sorting a list of conference attendees by country, click on a cell within the "Country" column.

3. **Sort Your Data**:
   - Go to the Data tab on the Ribbon.
   - Find the Sort & Filter group.
   - Select either Sort A to Z or Sort Z to A, depending on your needs.

Excel immediately reorders your data based on the selected column. The direct approach means that you don't have to go through multiple dialogs or settings, making it a quick method to get results.

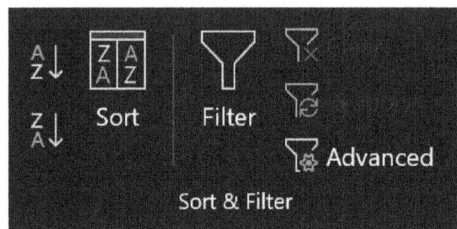

Practical Tip:

Always ensure that your headers are formatted differently from the rest of your data (e.g., bold text) and that the My data has headers option is selected. This prevents your headers from being mistaken for regular data during sorting operations.

Multi-Level Sorting

Multi-level sorting steps in when you need a more nuanced organization of your data. Suppose you wanted to organize the conference attendee list first by country and then by profession within each country. This detailed sorting allows you to analyze the representation of professions on a country-by-country basis.

Setting Up Multi-Level Sorting

1. **Prepare and Review Your Data**: As with single-level sorting, it's critical that your data is clearly divided into columns with headers.

2. **Accessing the Sort Dialog**:
   o Select any cell in the data range you want to sort.
   o Go to the Data tab.
   o Click on Sort in the Sort & Filter group to open the Sort dialog box.

3. **Adding Levels**:
   o In the Sort dialog, you'll see options for adding levels under Sort by.
   o Choose the primary column for your first level (e.g., "Country").
   o To add another level, click on Add Level, then choose the second column you want to sort by (e.g., "Profession").

4. **Configuring Each Level**:
   o For each level, decide whether you want ascending or descending order.
   o You can customize the sorting even further by clicking on Order and selecting Custom List if you have specific requirements (e.g., sorting days of the week in their chronological order).

5. **Executing the Sort**:
   o After setting up your levels and order, click OK.
   o Excel will now sort your data first by the primary level and then within that by the secondary level.

Practical Tip:

When performing multi-level sorts, it's useful to have a backup of your data or utilize the Undo feature (Ctrl + Z) immediately after sorting to prevent any accidental misplacement of data.

Real-World Example

Let's apply what you've learned with a practical example. Imagine you're managing staffing data and need to organize it by department and then by employee surname. By setting a multi-level sort, you can view all employees in each department alphabetically by their last name. This organization could enhance your ability to manage departmental resources and identify staffing needs more effectively.

Sorting in Excel can transform raw data into a structured format that's ripe for analysis and decision-making. Single-level sorting gives you quick insights, while multi-level sorting provides a deeper, more nuanced perspective.

Each step you take to learn and apply these sorting techniques builds your confidence in managing and interpreting data, turning you into a proficient and Excel-savvy professional. Remember, the key to mastering Excel lies in practicing these skills in real-world scenarios, so I encourage you to take any set of data and try these sorting methods to see the powerful impact they can have.

FILTERING DATA: AUTOFILTER, ADVANCED FILTERS

Filtering is akin to being the director of your data epic—you call the shots on what stays on screen and what gets cut. This functionality in Excel lets you focus on relevant information specific to your current needs, akin to zooming in with a camera to capture a subject's detailed expression among a bustling crowd. Here, we'll explore the two primary methods of filtering: AutoFilter and Advanced Filters, equipping you with the techniques to manage and analyze your data efficiently.

AutoFilter: Your Data's Gatekeeper

Imagine you're handed a list containing thousands of sales transactions from across the country, and you need to view only those that pertain to a specific region—say, the Northwest. Sifting through it manually would be overwhelming, akin to finding a needle in a haystack. That's when AutoFilter comes to your rescue, enabling you to view only the data that meets certain criteria.

How to Set Up AutoFilter

1. **Prepare Your Dataset**: Your data should be organized in rows and columns, with the first row serving as the header.
2. **Enabling AutoFilter**:
    o   Click on any cell in your data range.
    o   Navigate to the Data tab and click on the Filter icon in the Sort & Filter group.

You'll notice dropdown arrows appearing next to each of your column headers. These are your new tools to control the visibility of your data.

3. **Applying a Filter**:
    o   Click the dropdown arrow next to the column header you want to filter by.
    o   You'll see a list of all unique entries in that column. Simply check the boxes next to the values you want to see and uncheck the ones you want to hide.
    o   Excel will instantly update to display only the rows that meet your criteria.

Tips for Using AutoFilter:

- **Text Filters**: Not just limited to checkboxes for data points, but also custom filters like "begins with" or "contains" can refine your text data searches.
- **Number Filters**: For numerical data, filters such as "greater than," "less than," or "between" can immensely streamline your analysis.
- **Date Filters**: Sorting data by periods such as days, weeks, or years helps in managing timelines effectively.

Advanced Filters: Beyond the Basics

While AutoFilter is excellent for basic filtering needs, Advanced Filters are your go-to when the requirements become more complex. For instance, if you need to combine multiple conditions or apply more sophisticated criteria, this powerful feature steps in, letting you delve deeper into data analysis like a seasoned detective poring over clues.

Setting Up Advanced Filters

1. **Criteria Range Setup**:
   - Above your dataset, allocate a few rows to define your criteria. This area is crucial as it dictates the rules of the filtering.
   - Clearly label the criteria cells with the same headers as your data columns.
2. **Inputting Criteria**:
   - Enter the conditions under the appropriate headers in your criteria range. You can specify multiple conditions for filtering. For example, under the "Sales" header, you might specify ">5000" to view transactions greater than $5000.
3. **Applying the Advanced Filter**:
   - Select a cell within your main data table.
   - Go to the Data tab, click on Advanced in the Sort & Filter group.
   - In the Advanced Filter dialog box, choose if you want to filter the list in place or copy to another location.
   - Specify the List range and Criteria range using the range selector icons.

Tips for Advanced Filters:

- **Multiple Criteria**: You can set multiple criteria for the same column using different rows in the criteria range—Excel treats this as an OR condition, showing rows that meet any criteria specified.

- **AND Conditions**: To set up AND conditions (where all conditions must be met), input all criteria on the same row.

Practical Example: Filter in Action

Suppose you are tasked with extracting data for an upcoming presentation. You have a list of client interactions over the year, and you need entries from certain regions like the Northwest and Southwest but only where sales exceeded $5000. This task can be swiftly managed by setting up an advanced filter with both these criteria.

The Power of Filtered Data

By mastering AutoFilter and Advanced Filters, you've added a powerful layer to your data management skills. Filters not only simplify what could be overwhelming and chaotic but also enhance your ability to derive coherent narratives from your data—a fundamental skill for effective decision-making. Whether you're preparing a report, forecasting trends, or just organizing large datasets, remember that filters are key tools in your Excel toolkit, making your workflow not only manageable but also more strategic.

DATA VALIDATION: RESTRICTING INPUTS, DROP-DOWN LISTS

Ensuring data integrity in Excel isn't just about filtering and sorting—sometimes, it's more about prevention than correction. Data validation is a proactive tool that restricts the type of data or the values that users can enter into a cell. Much like setting the ground rules before a game, it ensures that everyone plays by the same set of guidelines, which in your case, helps maintain the accuracy and consistency of your data.

Restricting Inputs

Imagine you are managing an inventory list. It's crucial that entries in certain cells adhere to predefined guidelines—perhaps quantities must be whole numbers, and product codes must follow a specific format. This is where setting restrictions comes into play, preventing errors right at the source.

How to Set Up Data Validation

1. **Select the Cells**: First, pinpoint the cells where you need to implement the rules. If you're setting the same rule for several cells, you can select them all at once.
2. **Open the Data Validation Dialog Box**:

- o Navigate to the Data tab on the Ribbon.
- o Click on 'Data Validation' in the 'Data Tools' group.

Data Validation ? ✕

[Settings] Input Message Error Alert

Validation criteria

A̲llow:

Any value ∨ ☑ Ignore blank

Data:

between ∨

☐ Apply these changes to all other cells with the same settings

C̲lear All | OK | Cancel

3. **Configure the Validation Criteria**:
   - o In the Settings tab of the dialog box, under the Allow dropdown menu, select the type of data you expect in the cell (e.g., whole number, decimal, list, date, time, text length).
   - o Depending on the criteria chosen, you can set further specifics. For example, if 'Whole number' is selected, you can define whether the cell should be greater than, less than, between, or equal to certain values.
   - o Input these specifics in the Minimum and Maximum boxes or in the formula box for custom validations.

4. **Custom Error Alerts**:
   - o Navigate to the 'Error Alert' tab.
   - o Here, you can configure a custom message that pops up when someone tries to input invalid data. This message not only prevents the wrong entry but also guides users immediately about the correct data format.

Practical Tip:

For critical data entries, combining data validation with conditional formatting can provide visual cues about the validity of the data entered, enhancing both its appearance and functional accuracy.

Creating Drop-Down Lists

Drop-down lists enhance data integrity by limiting choices available to the user, making it a user-friendly way to control data input. Think of it as providing a menu in a restaurant—it simplifies the choice process and ensures that the kitchen prepares only what's available.

Step-by-Step Guide to Creating Drop-Down Lists

1. **Select the Cell**:
   - Choose the cell where you want the drop-down list.
2. **Access the Data Validation Settings**:
   - Similar to restricting inputs, go to the Data tab and select 'Data Validation'.
3. **Setting Up the List**:
   - In the Settings tab, choose List from the Allow options.
   - In the Source box, enter the values you want to appear in the list separated by commas, or select the range in the worksheet that contains the values you want to include.
4. **Finalizing and Testing Your Drop-Down**:
   - After inputting your desired options, click OK.
   - Click on the cell with your new drop-down list and a little arrow should appear on the right side of the cell. Click this arrow to see your list of options.

Practical Tip:

For dynamic drop-down lists that update as you add new entries to your data range, use a named range or a table for your list options. This way, as your table grows, your drop-down list will automatically include new entries.

Implementing Validation in Real-World Scenarios

Let's consider you're setting up a project tracking sheet. You can use drop-down lists for project status (e.g., Pending, In Progress, Completed) ensuring uniform data entries. Additionally, use data validation for date entries to ensure no past dates are entered for upcoming tasks.

Data validation in Excel serves as your frontline defense, preventing data entry errors before they can even happen. By walking through how to set up both simple restrictions and drop-down lists, we've equipped you with tools to ensure your data remains clean and dependable, paving the way for accurate analyses and wise decision-making.

Remember, valuing accuracy in your data collection methods isn't just about having clean data; it's about setting up a strong foundation for all your Excel tasks.

PREVENTING ERRORS: CIRCULAR REFERENCES AND FORMULA AUDITING

In the realm of Excel, precision is key, and the ability to preempt and resolve errors can significantly elevate your proficiency and confidence in handling data. When formulas go awry, they can produce misleading results and cause frustration. Today, we'll focus on preventing and addressing one of the most puzzling issues in Excel: circular references, along with the vital practice of formula auditing to keep your worksheets error-free and functionally robust.

Understanding Circular References

Imagine you are tasked with keeping a ledger in Excel. You set up a formula to sum up all the expenses to monitor monthly spending. By mistake, you include the total cell itself as a part of the range to be summed. Suddenly, Excel starts acting like a dog chasing its tail, because the total depends on itself to be calculated—this is a circular reference.

Circular references occur when a formula refers back to its own cell, either directly or through a series of formulas, which creates an infinite loop. While Excel usually flags this issue with a warning, understanding how to spot and resolve these can save you a headache.

How to Resolve Circular References

1. **Locate the Error**: Upon encountering a circular reference, Excel typically displays a warning message. Click on it, and Excel will take you to the problematic cell.
2. **Analyze the Formula**: Examine the formula in the formula bar. Look for any instance where the cell references include the cell where the formula is located.
3. **Correct the Reference**: Adjust the formula so that it no longer includes the cell itself or any other cell that leads back to the original in a loop.

Preventing circular references by double-checking formulas before entering them is a good practice, especially in complex worksheets with numerous calculations.

Formula Auditing: Your Data Quality Compass

Formula auditing is another indispensable tool in your Excel toolkit, designed to help you trace and debug formulas in your spreadsheets. It ensures accuracy in your calculations and helps you understand the relationships and dependencies among various cells.

Exploring Formula Auditing Tools

Excel offers several tools under the "Formula Auditing" group on the "Formulas" tab, each serving a specific purpose:

- **Trace Precedents**: This tool draws arrows from the cells that provide the data used in the selected formula. It's invaluable for understanding where the input values are coming from.
- **Trace Dependents**: Conversely, this shows where the output of the selected cell is being used across the workbook. It helps identify what might be affected if you change the current cell's value.
- **Remove Arrows**: Clears the arrows drawn by the Trace commands for a cleaner view once you're done checking.
- **Evaluate Formula**: Opens a dialog box that lets you see how a formula is calculated, step by step. This is particularly useful for breaking down complex formulas into understandable parts.

Step-by-Step Guide to Using Formula Auditing

1. **Select the Cell**: Click on the cell whose formula you need to audit.
2. **Trace Precedents/Dependents**: Click on either 'Trace Precedents' or 'Trace Dependents' to visualize the relationships.
3. **Remove Arrows**: Once you're done, clear the traces to keep your sheet neat.
4. **Evaluate Formula**: If the formula is still not working as expected, go to 'Evaluate Formula'. This tool will walk you through the formula execution, showing exactly how Excel arrives at the result, which can help pinpoint errors.

Implementing the Techniques

Consider you're analyzing a mid-year financial report and need to ensure all formulas calculating profit margins are accurate. By using the Trace Dependents tool, you identify not just the primary calculations but also other areas like projected year-end totals that are impacted by these margins. By mastering circular references and diving deep into formula auditing, you not only enhance your troubleshooting skills but also ensure your Excel workbooks are robust, accurate, and reliable. These practices are not just about fixing errors—they empower you to build complex, error-free models that stand strong under scrutiny and perform flawlessly, bolstering your reputation as a proficient Excel user. Keep these tools at your fingertips, and watch your confidence and credibility soar as you maneuver through Excel's challenges with ease.

CHAPTER 6: PIVOT TABLES AND DATA ANALYSIS

Imagine stepping into a bustling market; the stalls are overflowing with an array of goods—from fresh fruits to vibrant textiles. But without a way to sort and categorize these items, finding what you need can be overwhelming. This is similar to working with massive datasets in Excel. Enter Pivot Tables: your ultimate tool for organizing and analyzing your data so you can find valuable insights as effortlessly as picking apples from a neatly arranged fruit stall.

In this chapter, we dive into the world of Pivot Tables and Data Analysis—an essential skill set that can dramatically enhance your efficiency and ability to make informed decisions. Pivot Tables help you summarize large sets of data, reveal patterns, and even answer complex queries with just a few clicks. Think of it as having an expert assistant who instantly knows which data points are crucial and presents them in an easy-to-understand format.

Creating a Pivot Table isn't just about dragging and dropping data; it's an art you'll master, enabling you to see beyond numbers and into the trends and stories they tell. For example, if you're managing sales data, Pivot Tables can show you which products are performing best in different regions, what time of year sales peak, and where you might need to adjust your focus.

Moreover, we'll explore how to customize your Pivot Tables for more specific tasks—such as grouping data into meaningful categories, using slicers to make your tables truly interactive, and even creating timelines that spotlight trends over periods. These are not just technical skills, but gateways to becoming more strategic in your job or business.

By the end of this chapter, you'll not only be comfortable using Pivot Tables but will also be equipped to leverage them for powerful data analysis. Whether for business insights, academic research, or managing personal projects, the knowledge you gain today will make you an indispensable part of any team.

Remember, every large dataset tells a story. And with Pivot Tables, you're not just reading these stories—you're bringing them to life. Let's get started and turn you into a fluent narrator of data tales.

CREATING AND CUSTOMIZING PIVOT TABLES

Creating and customizing Pivot Tables in Excel isn't just a task—it's an adventure in unearthing the hidden potential within your data. Whether you're preparing business reports or organizing large datasets for personal projects, understanding how to effectively use Pivot Tables will revolutionize the way you handle and view your data.

Step 1: Getting Started with Pivot Tables

First things first: let's lay the foundation. To create a Pivot Table, you need a dataset to work from. This dataset should be organized in a table format, with rows and columns clearly labeled. The data could be anything from sales records, project timelines, or even personal expenses.

To create a Pivot Table, highlight your entire dataset, then navigate to the 'Insert' tab and select 'PivotTable'. Excel will ask where you want the Pivot Table to be placed. You can choose a new worksheet or a specific location in an existing sheet. For beginners, I recommend placing it in a new worksheet to keep things simple and tidy.

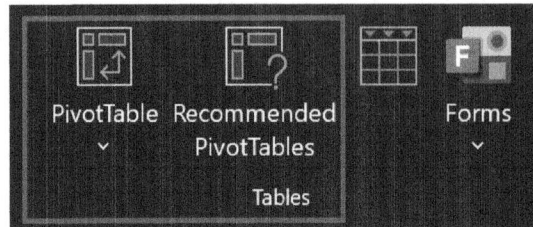

Step 2: Adding Fields to the Pivot Table

Once your blank Pivot Table is set up, you'll see a field list pane on the right side of your screen. This pane lists all the column labels from your original dataset. Here, you will decide what to pull into your Pivot Table. Your choices include:

- **Rows and Columns**: What do you want to analyze? Drag different fields to the 'Rows' and 'Columns' areas. For example, if you're handling sales data, you might place 'Product Category' as a Row and 'Quarter' as a Column to view sales by product across different quarters.

- **Values**: This area is where your numerical data makes an appearance. If continuing with the sales example, dragging 'Revenue' to the Values area will summarize the data, typically by summing or counting.

- **Filters**: To gain dynamic insights, you might add filters. If you're only interested in data from a particular region, drag 'Region' to the 'Filters' area. This allows you to focus or exclude parts of your data during analysis.

Step 3: Customizing Data Calculations

By default, Excel might summarize your data by summing values, but Pivot Tables offer much more. By clicking on the small arrow next to your value field in the Pivot Table Field List, you can access 'Value Field Settings'. Here you can choose how your data is calculated: sum, average, maximum, minimum, and more. Select what makes sense for the insight you are trying to obtain.

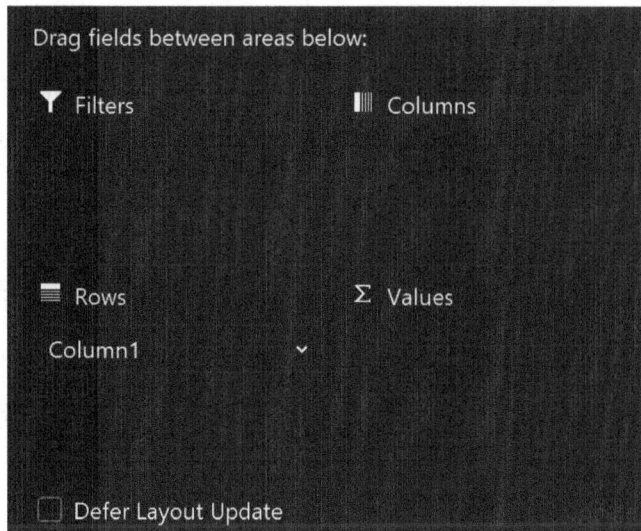

Step 4: Refreshing and Updating Your Pivot Table

One crucial aspect of using Pivot Tables effectively is ensuring they reflect the most current data. As you add more data to your original dataset, your Pivot Table won't automatically update. Right-click anywhere within the Pivot Table and select 'Refresh' to update the data within the Pivot Table according to any changes in the dataset.

Step 5: Making Your Pivot Table Interactive

Adding slicers can turn your static Pivot Table into an interactive dashboard. Slicers are visual filters. By adding a slicer, for instance, linked to the 'Region' field, users can press different regions displayed in the slicer to quickly see the data change within the Pivot Table based on the selected region.

To add a slicer, go to the PivotTable Analyze tab, and select 'Insert Slicer'. Choose the fields for which you want slicers, and position them near your Pivot Table for easy access.

Step 6: Visual Enhancements

Visuals aid in quick data analysis and make your data more appealing. Customize the look of your Pivot Table through the PivotTable Design tab. Choose from various styles and colors to differentiate your data clearly. Applying banded rows and columns, which alternate the background color of your data, can enhance readability.

Step 7: Drill Down for Details

Sometimes, seeing aggregated data isn't enough—you need to explore what makes up those numbers. Double-clicking on any data point within your Pivot Table allows you to see a detailed sheet of all the rows that contribute to that particular number. This is particularly handy when dealing with anomalies or outliers in your data.

Pivot Tables are not just a feature; they are a powerful tool that can provide profound insights and save tremendous time. Once you get the hang of it, you'll discover that creating and customizing Pivot Tables is a straightforward process. It helps transform extensive, complex data sets into manageable, understandable chunks of information, empowering you to make informed decisions based on substantive data analysis.

By incorporating these techniques into your daily work, you not only enhance your productivity but also become adept at handling one of Excel's most robust features. With each dataset you explore, you'll find yourself diving deeper into the realm of data possibilities that Pivot Tables offer.

Remember, each step brings you closer to mastering Excel and leveraging its full potential to benefit your projects, career, or personal data management efforts.

PIVOT CHARTS: ENHANCING DATA VISUALIZATION

When you visualize data, it transcends mere numbers and becomes a story—a narrative of peaks, valleys, trends, and insights waiting to be understood. Pivot Charts in Excel are your storytellers. They transform the data from your Pivot Tables into visual narratives, making complex analyses instantly more comprehensible and actionable. Let's embark on the journey of integrating Pivot Charts to enhance your data presentations, ensuring your data doesn't just speak but sings.

Beginning with Pivot Charts

If you've followed the steps to create a Pivot Table, generating a Pivot Chart is a natural next step. Here's why: while Pivot Tables are superb for analyzing and breaking down data, Pivot Charts enhance this analysis by adding the clarity and appeal of visual representation. To create a Pivot Chart, simply select your Pivot Table, navigate to the 'PivotTable Analyze' tab, and click on 'PivotChart'. Excel presents you with a variety of chart types to choose from—whether bar, line, pie, or area chart, select one that best suits the data story you are telling.

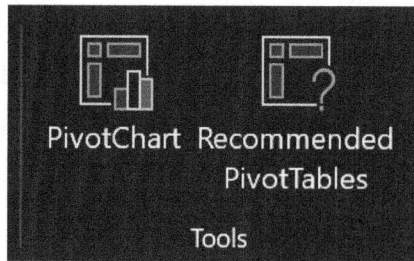

Selecting the Right Chart Type

Choosing the right type of chart is critical. Each chart variant paints a different picture:

- **Column and Bar Charts**: Ideal for comparing the frequency, count, or value of items across different categories.
- **Line Charts**: Perfect for illustrating trends over time.
- **Pie Charts**: Useful for showing proportions within a whole.
- **Area Charts**: Best suited for displaying the magnitude of trends over time, layered with multiple data series.

Tip: Always align your chart choice with the kind of story you want the data to tell. Is it about growth, distribution, or proportion? Each story has a matching chart.

Customizing Your Pivot Charts

A chart's impact lies in its ability to convey information clearly and promptly. Customization can significantly enhance this. Here's how you can tailor your Pivot Charts:

1. **Design and Layout**: Access these options under the 'Chart Tools' in the ribbon. Here, you can modify chart styles, colors, and layouts. Professional and clean visuals make your data stand out and become more digestible.
2. **Chart Titles and Labels**: Always include a clear, descriptive title. Also, make use of axis titles and data labels to ensure that someone viewing the chart can easily understand what each component represents without guessing.
3. **Slicers for Interactive Charts**: Just like with Pivot Tables, adding slicers to Pivot Charts allows viewers to interact with the data. This feature lets them focus on specific filters without altering the structure of the chart. It's particularly useful during presentations or when sharing reports.

Linking Pivot Charts and Tables for Deeper Insights

One of the strengths of Pivot Charts lies in their connection to Pivot Tables. Any change you make in the Pivot Table, like filtering or sorting data, is instantly reflected in the corresponding Pivot Chart. This dynamic relationship ensures consistency and accuracy in your data stories.

Imagine presenting sales data over the past year, broken down by quarters and product categories. Your Pivot Table organizes the sales numbers neatly, and your Pivot Chart shows trends over time with peaks and dips. Suddenly, your quarterly review meeting is not just about tables of numbers, but a clear visual story of what went well and what didn't.

Navigating Common Pitfalls

While Pivot Charts are powerful, they have nuances that, if ignored, can lead to misinterpretation:

- **Over-Cluttering**: Too many data series in one chart can confuse rather than clarify. Simplify by focusing only on key data points.
- **Wrong Chart Type**: Using an inappropriate chart type can lead to incorrect interpretations of data. Always match your data's narrative to the chart type.
- **Ignoring Design Essentials**: A well-designed chart conveys data more effectively. Pay attention to color contrasts, font sizes, and the overall readability of the chart.

Using Pivot Charts Effectively

To use Pivot Charts effectively, consider your audience and the key message you want to communicate. Here are a few scenarios:

- **For Executives**: Summarize key trends and growth metrics with clean, high-level charts.
- **For Teams**: Use more detailed charts to dive deep into specific areas like productivity metrics or project timelines.
- **For Stakeholders**: Create interactive charts with slicers so they can explore the data points that matter most to them.

Pivot Charts transform raw data into visual insights that communicate stories hidden within extensive spreadsheets. They not only support data analysis but enhance it, making complex patterns and trends understandable at a glance. As you craft your Pivot Charts, remember that each element of your chart is part of a larger narrative. Let your data tell its story compellingly and correctly, ensuring that your work not only informs but also inspires action.

By mastering Pivot Charts, you don't just become proficient in a tool; you become a storyteller who uses data to narrate compelling, insightful tales. And in the world of Excel, where data speaks volumes, being able to tell its story effectively is an unparalleled skill.

GROUPING, SLICERS, AND TIMELINES IN PIVOT TABLES

In the rich tapestry of data analysis that Excel offers, some features are like the hidden threads that, when pulled, reveal a new dimension of patterns and insights. Grouping, Slicers, and Timelines are precisely such features in Pivot Tables. They bring a level of granularity and interactivity to your data analysis tasks, allowing for a dynamic exploration that goes beyond static tables and charts.

Understanding Grouping in Pivot Tables

Grouping in Pivot Tables is akin to organizing a cluttered desk into neatly labeled folders. It enhances clarity and focus by allowing you to segment your data into meaningful categories or ranges. For instance, consider you have sales data spanning several years. Without grouping, analyzing this data can be cumbersome. By grouping data by years, quarters, or months, you're structuring it in a way that allows for quick, comparative insights across different time periods.

Using Grouping Effectively

Let's say your dataset includes individual transaction dates. While useful, this level of detail can make it hard to see broader trends. Here's how you can group these dates into months and years in your Pivot Table:

1. Right-click on any date in your Pivot Table.
2. Select 'Group' from the contextual menu.
3. In the 'Group' dialog box, choose how you want to group your data—by months, quarters, or years. You can even select multiple grouping criteria to compile your data more comprehensively.

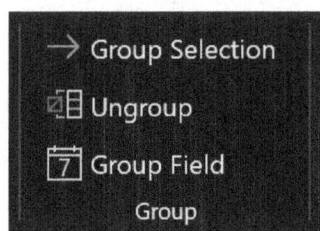

Grouping isn't limited to dates. Numeric fields can also be grouped to create ranges that might be more relevant for your analysis.

For example, grouping customer age data into brackets (e.g., 18-25, 26-35, etc.) can provide clearer insights into which age groups are most engaged with your product.

Enhancing Interactivity with Slicers

While filters in Pivot Tables are useful, they aren't the most intuitive for rapid, on-the-fly changes, especially during presentations or collaborative meetings. This is where Slicers come into play. They add a visual element to filtering, making interactivity as straightforward as clicking on a beautifully designed button.

Implementing Slicers

Adding a Slicer is simple:

1. Click anywhere inside your Pivot Table to activate the PivotTable Tools in the ribbon.
2. Go to the 'Analyze' tab and select 'Insert Slicer'.
3. Choose the fields for which you'd like to create Slicers. For instance, adding a Slicer for 'Region' allows users to quickly view data for selected geographical areas without navigating complex filter menus.

Slicers not only simplify data filtering but also enhance the visual appeal of your data presentation, making the interaction seamless and intuitive. They are particularly useful in dashboards and reports where non-technical stakeholders need to dive into the data.

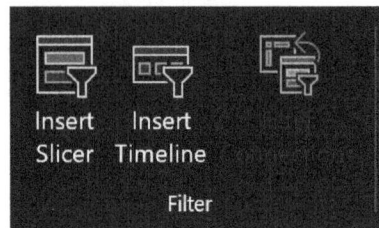

Timelines: A Visualization Tool for Date Fields

Timelines are a specific type of Slicer specially designed for date fields. They provide a more granular approach to filtering by dates, offering an intuitive, graphical way to drill down into periods of time—be it years, quarters, months, or even days.

Adding a Timeline to Your Pivot Table

Here's how you can integrate a Timeline:

1. Ensure your Pivot Table includes a field with date values.
2. Click on 'Insert Timeline' in the 'Analyze' tab.
3. Select the date field you want to use, and a sleek, interactive Timeline will appear.

Now, you can select specific periods with a simple swipe or click, dynamically updating the associated Pivot Table data.

Timelines not only make your reports look more sophisticated but also offer an unparalleled ease of use, making it a breeze to navigate through time periods.

The Synergy of Grouping, Slicers, and Timelines

When used together, Grouping, Slicers, and Timelines transform your Pivot Tables from static tables into dynamic, interactive data exploration tools. This synergy allows you to: - Quickly adapt data views to different audiences or questions. - Enhance the interactivity of reports, making them user-friendly and visually appealing. - Deliver personalized insights by easily slicing through data layers.

By incorporating Grouping, Slicers, and Timelines into your Pivot Tables, you're not just analyzing data; you're weaving it into a narrative that can be tailored at the touch of a button. These tools empower you to present complex data in understandable segments, cater to varied analytical needs, and engender a proactive approach to data exploration.

In essence, mastering these tools equips you with the capability to not only respond to but also anticipate the questions that arise in data-driven discussions. It positions you as not just a data analyst but as a data strategist, harnessing Excel's robust features to drive decisions and strategies grounded in solid, interactively presented evidence.

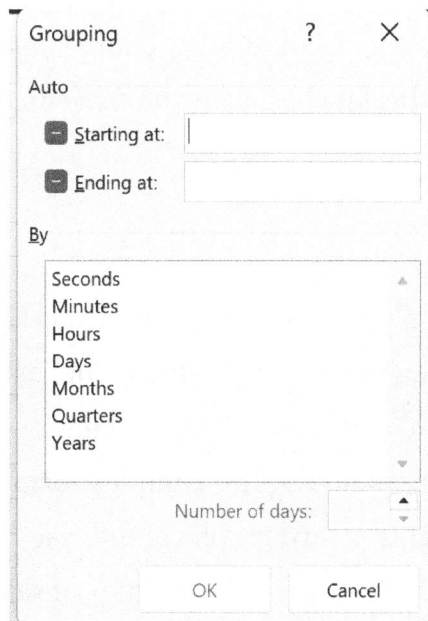

AUTOMATING REPORTS WITH POWER QUERY

In our digital age, data is not just a part of our lives—it **is** our lives, encompassing everything from business operations to personal budget tracking. But managing this data, especially big data that accumulates over time from multiple sources, can be daunting.

This brings us to a magical tool in Excel called **Power Query**, a game-changer for automating the processes of importing, transforming, and integrating data into your reports.

Imagine you're tasked with a monthly report that requires gathering data from various formats and sources, transforming it, and then consolidating it into a comprehensive report. Doing this manually every month is not only time-consuming but also prone to errors. Power Query simplifies this by automating the whole process. It's like setting up a domino effect; you arrange everything meticulously once, and then with a single flick, everything aligns automatically thereafter.

Streamlining Data Import with Power Query

Power Query is your go-to tool for connecting to external data sources—from simple Excel sheets and CSV files to more complex databases like SQL, and even data from web pages. It offers a user-friendly interface where you can select the source, and it fetches the data for you.

This can be particularly handy when dealing with data that's regularly updated at its source because Power Query can refresh the data based on your specified frequency, keeping your reports up-to-date with minimal effort.

Transforming Data with Ease

Once data is imported, it often isn't in the format you need. Here's where Power Query excels, allowing you to transform this data using simple steps. For instance, you might need to remove certain columns, filter rows, split data into different columns, or merge data from different sources. Traditionally, these tasks would require complex formulas or macros, but Power Query makes these accessible via a straightforward graphical interface.

Imagine you're handling sales data where the date and time of sales are in one column. With Power Query, you can easily split this into two separate columns, one for date and one for time, enhancing your analysis capability without writing a single line of code.

Merging and Appending Queries

Often, data isn't just spread across formats but also across multiple datasets. For example, you might have sales data in one table and customer demographic data in another. Power Query allows you to merge these tables using a common key, similar to a VLOOKUP in Excel, but more powerful. Alternatively, if you have data that spans multiple periods stored in separate files but with the same structure, Power Query can append these into a single table, streamlining the process significantly.

This merging and appending functionality is not just a convenience; it's a powerhouse capability. It ensures that your data is not just collected but also connected, giving you insights that are not possible with isolated datasets.

Automating Data Refresh

One of Power Query's most compelling features is its ability to automate data refreshes. Once you have set up a query—defined the source, specified the transformations, and outlined how data should be merged—you can instruct Power Query to refresh the data at regular intervals automatically. This means your monthly report can literally prepare itself while you focus on what the data is telling you, not how you get it.

Consider a scenario where you are tracking market trends, and data is updated every day. With Power Query, you can set your workbook to refresh daily, pulling in the updated data automatically. Every morning, your report is ready with the latest figures, no manual intervention required.

Integration with Pivot Tables

The processed data from Power Query can be seamlessly integrated into Pivot Tables, marrying the robust analytical capabilities of Pivot Tables with the dynamic data handling of Power Query. This integration allows for an almost cinematic transformation of raw data into insightful, actionable information.

Advanced Data Transformation

For those who love diving deep, Power Query supports advanced data modeling techniques. You can create custom functions, apply conditional logic, and even integrate R or Python scripts. These capabilities open up a realm where data handling becomes truly limitless.

Power Query: The Workflow Enhancer

With Power Query, the workflow of importing, cleaning, and preparing data is not just optimized but also set on a schedule that runs with precision. It's about making the data work for you and not the other way around. This tool not only saves time but also ensures that your data reports are robust, accurate, and always up-to-date.

In summary, Power Query is not merely a feature within Excel; it's a transformational tool that, once harnessed, can significantly elevate your proficiency in handling big data. It's akin to having a skilled assistant dedicated to data management, available at the click of a button.

For anyone looking to streamline their data processes and focus more on analysis than data prep, mastering Power Query is not just beneficial; it's essential.

Chapter 7: Creating Effective Charts and Graphs

Have you ever found yourself staring at a spreadsheet filled with data, feeling completely lost on how to showcase it? Well, you're not alone. This is where the art of visualization comes into play, turning those daunting datasets into clear, compelling visuals. Today, in our journey through Excel, we land on a crucial skill every Excel user must master—creating effective charts and graphs. Imagine you're at a crucial meeting, armed with your Excel charts that not only look stunning but also tell a compelling story of the data. You plot trends over time, compare sales figures, or maybe highlight budget allocations—and with each graph, your audience's understanding deepens. That's the power of well-crafted visuals; they can make complex information accessible and engaging.

In this chapter, we're diving into the various types of charts available in Excel. Each type serves a unique purpose. For example, a line chart is perfect for showing trends over time, whereas a pie chart offers a clear visual of proportions. But, it's not just about choosing the right type of chart; it's also about customizing it to enhance readability and impact. From tweaking the color schemes to adjusting the axis labels, these little details can dramatically improve how your charts communicate the underlying data.

We'll also explore some sophisticated aspects of chart customization like adding trendlines, which can provide insights into data trends at a glance, and inserting secondary axes, allowing us to compare different datasets on the same graph. These tools are not just about making your charts look good—they're about making them a powerful analysis tool.

As we proceed, remember, the goal here isn't just to learn how to create charts, but to understand how to use them as a narrative tool in business and beyond. By the end of this chapter, you'll be equipped not only to transform numbers into visually engaging charts but also to tell your data's story in a way that captures attention and drives your points home. Let's make your data not just seen, but understood.

Choosing the Right Chart Type (Bar, Line, Pie, Combo)

Selecting the right chart type might seem straightforward at first—just a matter of choosing the prettiest option, right? But the truth is, choosing effectively hinges on what your data aims to communicate. Let's walk through the essential chart types—Bar, Line, Pie, and Combo—and unravel when and why each type should be your go-to option.

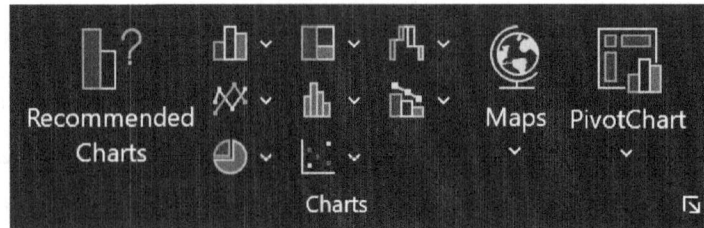

Bar Charts

Ah, the trusty bar chart—ideal for showing comparisons among categories. Imagine you own a chain of cafes in different cities, and you're comparing the monthly sales across these locations.

A bar chart will allow your stakeholders to see at a glance which locations are outperforming or underperforming. Each bar represents a different locality, and its length indicates the sales volume—simple yet effective.

Now, suppose you're interested in seeing sales data not just by locality, but also by product type within each location. Here, the stacked bar chart comes into play. It breaks down each bar into segments that represent different products, offering a layered understanding of what's selling where.

But what if your data involves changes over a small period and includes negative values? This is a job for the horizontal bar chart. Let's say your cafe chain had a sudden influx of returns or unsold perishables. A horizontal bar, with bars extending to the left for returns and to the right for sales, would cleanly showcase this balance (or imbalance).

Line Charts

Line charts are the go-to when you want to track changes over time—perfect for trends. Imagine tracking the same cafe sales, but now you're not just measuring the 'what' but the 'when'. Prices fluctuate, marketing campaigns come and go, and seasons change. A line chart can help you visualize sales trends over the months or years, displaying peaks and troughs in a way that's instantly understandable.

Suppose you're also running a loyalty program, and you want to measure its effectiveness over time alongside your sales data. A multi-line chart can track multiple data streams, like sales and loyalty sign-ups, on the same graph. Each line represents a different dataset, allowing for a direct visual comparison of how different factors relate over time.

Pie Charts

When it comes to showing parts of a whole, pie charts shine. They give a quick snapshot of proportions and are intuitive to read—everyone loves a good pie, after all. Let's say you want to distribute your annual budget across various departments. A pie chart can help you show at a glance how much of your total budget goes to marketing, procurement, staffing, etc., emphasizing shares in a visually digestible format.

But beware, pie charts have their limitations. When there are too many categories or when the values are too close, pies can become confusing. In such cases, other charts, such as bar charts, might be clearer.

Combo Charts

When you need to communicate complex datasets with dual emphasis—such as correlating different but related data types—a combo chart comes into its own. Consider you want to analyze both the quantity of coffee beans sold and the revenue generated. These are inherently correlated but different data types—one being units sold (a simple count) and the other revenue (a dollar amount).

A combo chart enables you to plot one dataset on a primary vertical axis (say, units sold as bars) and another on a secondary vertical axis (revenue as a line). This dual-axis approach allows for a nuanced analysis within a single graphical framework, providing a layered narrative about how various aspects of your business impact each other.

Practical Tips:

- **Consistency is Key:** When creating a series of charts, keep your design consistent. Use the same color scheme, label style, and layout. This consistency will make your presentations look professional and help your audience focus on the data, not the differences in design.
- **Less is More:** Don't overcrowd your charts. Over-plotting makes charts less readable. Aim for simplicity to help your audience quickly grasp the essentials.
- **Annotate Wisely:** Use annotations to highlight key insights or unusual values in your data. This draws attention where it's most needed.

By understanding the strengths and best applications of each chart type, you can transform standard Excel spreadsheets into effective storytelling tools—making your data not just seen, but understood and actionable. Whether through bar, line, pie, or combo charts, the goal is always to shed the best light on your data, enhancing your capability to make informed, impactful decisions.

CUSTOMIZING CHART ELEMENTS: AXIS, LABELS, LEGENDS

Customizing the various elements of your charts can turn a standard visualization into a clear, effective communication tool. Let's delve into how tweaking axes, labels, and legends can optimize the readability and impact of your charts. This will help ensure your visuals not only capture attention but also convey the intended insights at a glance.

Axis Customization

Every chart tells a story, and the axes are the backbone of that narrative. Properly adjusted axes can emphasize important data points and facilitate better understanding of trends.

1. **Scaling Your Axes**: The first aspect to consider is the scale of your axes—too wide a scale can make differences in data less perceptible, while too narrow a range might exaggerate minor fluctuations. Imagine plotting yearly revenue where one aberrant year distorts the scale so much that other variations become indiscernible. Adjusting the scale to more closely fit the range of your typical data gives a more accurate year-over-year comparison.

2. **Choosing the Right Intervals**: Set intervals that make sense for your data and audience. For a financial analyst, a graph that increments by thousands might be perfect, but for a presentation to stakeholders not familiar with the specifics, rounding off to nearest tens could simplify understanding without loss of key insights.

3. **Formatting Axis Labels**: Legibility is crucial. Ensure your axis labels are clear and not too dense. Rotate labels if they're crowding each other or use a smaller font that remains readable. A small format tweak can prevent misinterpretations or confusion.,

Label Customization

Labels provide your chart with context. From data labels within a bar chart that show exact values to axis titles that explain what each dimension represents, clear labels are indispensable.

1. **Direct Data Labels**: There are situations where data labels can be more effective than a legend, particularly in pie charts or stacked bar charts where viewing exact values at a glance aids comprehension. For instance, in a pie chart showing market share, direct labels on each 'slice' allow for immediate comparison without back-and-forth referencing to a legend.

2. **Axis Titles and Chart Title**: Never overlook the power of a well-named chart and axes. These elements tell your audience what they are looking at without needing additional context from the presenter.

The axis titles should accurately reflect the units of measurement and variables, while a succinct chart title guides the viewer on the chart's purpose.

Legend Customization

Legends help decode the chart, but a poorly placed or styled legend can clutter your visual or confuse viewers.

1. **Positioning the Legend**: Often, the default position is at the right or bottom. However, if placing the legend there causes overlap or distracts from important data, consider moving it. In Excel, you can easily drag the legend to a different position. The top or a side margin might be better alternatives depending on your specific chart's layout and data density.

2. **Deciding When to Use (or Not Use) a Legend**: For simpler graphs or charts with direct labeling, a legend may be redundant. Assess whether each element of your chart is adding value. If a legend only repeats what's already clear from the labels, it might be better to remove it entirely for a cleaner look.

3. **Styling for Clarity**: Ensure your legend is as minimal as necessary to be understood—match the color and style with the chart for a unified look. Consistency in font, color, and spacing contributes significantly to a professional and easy-to-read presentation.

Practical Tips:

- **Test Different Styles**: Sometimes, what works in theory doesn't pan out in practice. Preview your chart with various customizations to see what best enhances clarity and aesthetics.

- **Feedback Loop**: Show your charts to others before finalizing them. Fresh eyes can often spot confusing elements or suggest improvements you might have missed.

- **Keep Learning**: Excel's capabilities are vast and regularly updated. Stay updated with new features that might offer even more sophisticated ways to customize and enhance your chart visualizations.

By tailoring these chart elements, your data visualization will not only carry more weight but also provide clearer, more immediate insights. Customizations like these empower you to guide your audience through the data as seamlessly and effectively as possible, ensuring your presentations achieve their intended effect.

ADDING TRENDLINES AND SECONDARY AXES

As we delve deeper into the world of Excel charts, it becomes evident that some features are particularly powerful for enhancing our ability to analyze and present data more effectively. Two such features that stand out are the use of trendlines and secondary axes in charts. These tools can provide additional layers of insight into your data, allowing you to communicate complex information smoothly and efficiently. Let's explore how these features can be applied to sharpen your data analysis and presentation skills.

Understanding and Adding Trendlines

Trendlines are critical when you need to illustrate the direction or tendency in a data set over a period. They help in identifying patterns, making forecasts, and getting a clear view of what future data might look like based on current trends.

Imagine you're analyzing quarterly sales data. Initially, the numbers alone might tell you only so much, but by adding a trendline, you suddenly visualize whether sales are growing, stagnant, or declining over time. This can be a game-changer in business presentations or strategic meetings where visual representations of trends can influence decision-making processes significantly.

To add a trendline in Excel, here's a simplified walkthrough:

1. **Choose Your Chart**: Primarily, trendlines are added to scatter plots and line charts. So, first ensure your data is visualized in one of these formats.

2. **Add the Trendline**: Click on the data series to which you want to add the trendline. Right-click and select 'Add Trendline' from the context menu. Excel offers several types of trendlines such as linear, exponential, and polynomial. Choose the one that best fits the pattern of your data.

3. **Customize Your Trendline**: Excel allows you to set specific options for your trendline like setting intercept, displaying the equation on the chart, and more, enabling you to tailor the trendline to meet your specific analytical needs.

The application of a trendline can transform a simple chart into a powerful forecast tool, especially when combined with Excel's forecasting features.

Incorporating Secondary Axes

When dealing with diverse datasets that vary widely in scale, utilizing a secondary axis in a chart lets you visualize the relationship between two different variables in a single graphic. This is particularly useful in scenarios where comparing these variables directly helps to draw meaningful insights that might not be apparent from isolated observation.

Consider you have data for ad spend and sales revenue over several months. Since the scale of budget spent and revenue generated could be vastly different, plotting them on the same chart without a secondary axis might make the trends in ad spend almost invisible. Introducing a secondary axis solves this problem by allowing each dataset to have its own scale on either side of the chart, making both trends readily analyzable.

Here's how to add a secondary axis to a chart in Excel:

1. **Create Your Chart**: Start with a standard chart, ideally a combo chart, where you intend to compare two different types of data.

2. **Add the Secondary Axis**: Click on the data series you wish to plot against a secondary axis. Then, under Chart Tools, select 'Format'. Click on 'Series Options', and then check the option for 'Secondary Axis'. You'll see the secondary scale appear on the right side of your chart.

3. **Adjust and Customize**: You might need to adjust the scale of your secondary axis for better visibility and comparison.

Ensure that the scales are not misleading but help clarify the relationship between the two data sets. Customize the axis titles to clearly indicate what each axis represents.

Practical Tips:

- **Use Trendlines Judiciously**: While trendlines can provide great insights, avoid overfitting lines to data that are inherently random or seasonal as it may lead to misleading interpretations.

- **Clearly Label Your Axes**: With the addition of a secondary axis, it becomes even more crucial to label your axes clearly to avoid confusion. Always indicate which data series corresponds to which axis.

- **Check for Scale Discrepancies**: When using secondary axes, ensure that the difference in scale does not distort the interpretation of data. The goal is to enhance understanding, not complicate it.

By mastering these advanced chart features in Excel, you can elevate the level of sophistication in your data analysis and presentations. Trendlines forecast and elucidate patterns, while secondary axes allow for a nuanced comparison of distinct but related datasets. Together, these tools empower you to deliver deeper insights and a more compelling data narrative.

INTERACTIVE DASHBOARDS: DYNAMIC CHARTS AND SLICERS

In the world of data, static charts and tables are like silent movies; effective up to a point but lacking the dynamic interaction that modern audiences crave. In contrast, interactive dashboards are your talkies. They offer viewers active engagement, allowing them to explore data through various lenses and levels of detail, transforming data analysis from a spectator sport into a hands-on experience. Learning how to build these dynamic charts and integrate slicers will elevate your Excel skills from proficient to powerhouse.

Dynamic Charts: Bringing Data to Life

A dynamic chart in Excel is one that adjusts automatically based on the specific subsets of data chosen for viewing. This means that as you filter or shift your data, the chart updates instantly to reflect just the set of data you're interested in at any moment.

For example, if you have a yearly sales chart, you could click through monthly or quarterly views within the same chart, bringing clarity to trends and anomalies over different periods without manually changing the dataset every time.

To create a dynamic chart, you start by setting up your data in a table format. This allows Excel to better manage and reference the data. You then create a standard chart using this table. The magic happens when you tie chart controls like form controls or slicers to this data table, enabling real-time updates of the content based on user interaction.

Slicers: Simplifying Data Manipulation

Slicers are powerful tools introduced in newer versions of Excel, designed for filtering table data or PivotTables. They present a visual way to add interactive filtering capabilities to your reports and dashboards. Unlike standard filters that are hidden behind drop-down menus, slicers are always on display, making it easy to see current filtering states at a glance.

Imagine you are analyzing a report containing several years of sales data across multiple regions. By adding slicers for both 'Year' and 'Region', you provide stakeholders the ability to instantly focus on what interests them. One can quickly view data from 2022 in North America, then with a single click, switch to Asia in 2019, all while maintaining visibility of the options available and active filters applied.

Building an Interactive Dashboard

Creating an interactive dashboard might sound daunting, but it's essentially about layering these elements — dynamic charts and slicers — in a coherent and user-friendly layout. Here's a simplified approach:

1. **Layout Your Dashboard**: Start by sketching out a rough layout, deciding where each chart, table, and slicer will go. Aim for a flow that matches the way users logically process information. For example, put slicers at the top or side as clear entry points for data interaction.

2. **Incorporate Charts and Tables**: Position your charts and tables based on the sketched layout. Make sure they are sized appropriately to not overwhelm each other, yet still deliver comprehensive information at a glance.

3. **Integrate Slicers**: Add slicers related to your datasets and connect them to your charts and tables. Align slicers neatly so that they complement the data visualizations rather than clutter the dashboard.

4. **Customize for Clarity**: Adjust colors, fonts, and styles in your dashboard for a clean and professional appearance. Consistency is key to avoiding visual confusion and ensuring that users can seamlessly interact with data.

5. **Test Interactivity**: Like rehearsing a play before the curtains rise, test your dashboard thoroughly. Interact with every element to ensure filters, charts, and tables respond as expected. An unresponsive or misleading dashboard can cause more frustration than a static report.

Think of building your first interactive dashboard as setting up a stage where your data is the star. The slicers are your stagehands, dynamic charts the scenery, all coming together to support a compelling, interactive performance that informs and engages your audience.

Practical Tips:

- **Keep it Intuitive**: Design with the end-user in mind. The dashboard should be intuitive enough for anyone in your organization to use, from the tech-savvy to those less familiar with data analysis tools.

- **Focus on Relevance**: Only include visuals that add value to the dashboard's purpose. Overloading with too many dynamic elements can distract from key insights.

- **Use Tooltips**: Employ tooltips effectively by providing brief descriptions or explanations that appear when users hover over elements of the dashboard. This helps guide less experienced users through the data exploration process.

Interactive dashboards empower users to explore and interact with data on their own terms, fostering a deeper understanding and retention of the information presented. In Excel, mastering the use of dynamic charts and slicers lays down the groundwork for creating these compelling, interactive environments.

Chapter 8: Automating Tasks with Macros and VBA

Welcome to Day 4 of our journey through Excel, where we've reached a pivotal moment—transforming routine tasks into time-saving triumphs using Macros and VBA. Perhaps you've spent hours, perhaps even days, manually performing tasks in Excel. You're aware that every repeated click is a slice of time you'll never get back. Imagine then a world where Excel does all that heavy lifting for you, where a single command triggers a sequence of actions flawlessly executed, freeing you up for those high-impact projects that really need your brain and creativity. We start our deep dive into automation by demystifying Macros. Think of a Macro as an efficient assistant—you show it precisely what to do once, and it repeats that exact sequence whenever called upon. From formatting reports to extracting data, Macros are a real game-changer in optimizing your productivity.

Venturing further into automation, we enter the realm of Visual Basic for Applications (VBA)—Excel's powerful scripting language that allows you to scale up your automation efforts. Here, we move from simple task replication to creating custom functionalities tailored to your specific needs. Whether it's developing complex algorithms for financial analysis or automating data entry processes, VBA provides the tools to create solutions that are not just about doing things faster, but smarter.

This chapter isn't just about learning; it's about empowering you to elevate your analytic capabilities, to innovate your workflow, and ultimately, to become a maestro of Excel automation. With VBA, you'll transcend ordinary tasks to solve real-world business problems with a level of sophistication and efficiency that sets you apart in any professional setting.

By the end of today, the mystical aura that may have surrounded the terms 'Macros' and 'VBA' will dissolve into clear, actionable knowledge. Get ready to replace tedium with automation, to replace dread with anticipation, as we unlock the full potential of Excel to work not just hard, but smart.

Introduction to Macros: Recording and Running Macros

Imagine, for a moment, diving into a treasure trove of Excel tips that transforms the way you work every day: that's the power of Macros. Macros in Excel are not just tools; they're your partners in the quest for efficiency, allowing you to automate repetitive tasks with a finesse that saves not only time but also ensures accuracy and consistency across your work. Today, we're going to demystify the process of creating and utilizing Macros, ensuring that every step is practical, clear, and immediately applicable.

Step 1: Understanding What Macros Are

First off, let's clear the air about what Macros really are – think of them as a series of instructions that you can program to execute tasks automatically in Excel. These could be as simple as formatting a report or as complex as pulling data from external databases and using it to populate your spreadsheet.

Step 2: Setting Up Your Excel Environment for Macros

Before you can start creating Macros, you need to make sure your Excel environment is set up to handle them. This means checking your settings to enable all features related to Macros:

- Go to the 'File' menu, click on 'Options', and then select 'Trust Center'.
- In the Trust Center menu, click on 'Trust Center Settings'.
- Navigate to the 'Macro Settings' and make sure the 'Enable all macros' and 'Trust access to the VBA project object model' options are selected.

This setup is crucial because Excel, by default, disables some capabilities for Macros to protect your computer from potentially unsafe code.

Step 3: Recording Your First Macro

Recording a Macro is remarkably straightforward in Excel. It's like telling Excel: "Watch me do this," and then Excel replicates it exactly. Here's how you can record your first Macro:

- Open a new Excel workbook to practice.
- Go to the 'View' tab, and in the 'Macros' group, click on 'Record Macro'.
- A dialog box appears. Here, you can name your Macro, add a description, and assign a shortcut key if you wish.
- Click 'OK' and carry out the tasks that you want to automate. This could be anything from formatting cells, inputting data, or setting up equations.
- Once you're done, return to the 'View' tab and click 'Stop Recording'.

Congratulations! You've created your first macro. You can now run this Macro in any workbook on your machine using the shortcut you assigned or by navigating to 'Macros' under the 'View' tab, where you can view, run, edit, or delete your Macros.

Step 4: Running Your Recorded Macro

Running a Macro is as simple as creating one:

- Go to the 'View' tab.
- Click on 'Macros', select 'View Macros'.
- You'll see a list of available Macros. Select the one you want to run and click 'Run'.

Instantly, Excel will execute all the steps you recorded.

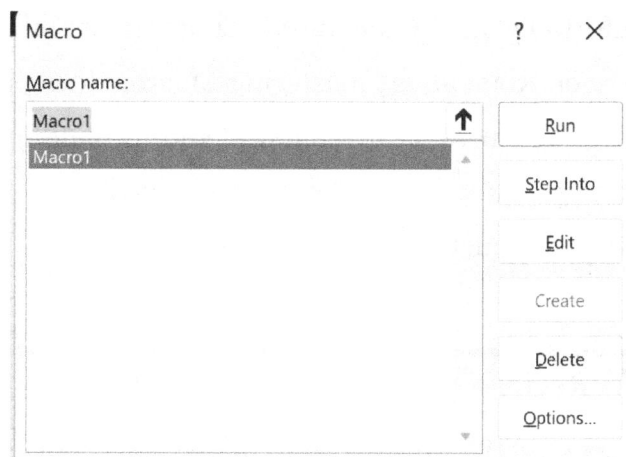

Step 5: Editing Your Macro

Sometimes, you might need to tweak your Macros for better performance or due to changes in your tasks. Editing a Macro, though, involves stepping into the world of VBA (Visual Basic for Applications), Excel's programming environment:

- Go to 'Macros', choose 'View Macros', select the Macro you want to edit, and click 'Edit'.
- This action opens the VBA editor, showing the code that Excel automatically generated when you recorded your Macro. Here, you can modify the code directly—but caution is advised if you're not familiar with basic programming concepts.

Step 6: Adding Practicality with Macro Tips

- **Organize Macros:** Keep your Macros organized by naming them clearly. This way, you know exactly what each Macro is for, making your work smoother.
- **Use Relative References:** When recording a Macro, consider using 'Use Relative References' if you want your Macro to work based on its current position in the spreadsheet, rather than the exact cells you select during the recording.
- **Test Your Macros:** Always test your Macros in a sample workbook to ensure they perform as expected without altering your important data.

Real-World Examples

Let's apply this to a real-world scenario. Imagine you're an analyst needing to format and analyze sales data monthly. Without Macros, you manually import, clean, and format data, taking considerable time and increasing the risk of errors. With Macros, all these steps can be automated, allowing you to focus more on analyzing the data and drawing insights, enhancing productivity and accuracy.

By now, you should comfortably grasp the initial creation, running, editing, and practical application of Macros in Excel. Remember, mastering Macros doesn't just augment your Excel skills; it amplifies your professional value by enabling you to handle data more efficiently and accurately. Embrace these steps, practice diligently, and watch as Excel starts working almost magically, well beyond simple spreadsheets.

BASIC VBA CODING: WRITING YOUR FIRST MACRO

Embarking on the journey of automating Excel through Basic VBA coding is like learning a new language. Just as a new language opens you up to a new world of communication, understanding VBA—or Visual Basic for Applications—unlocks a new realm of efficiency and capability in how you manage data and perform tasks in Excel.

The Promise of VBA

In Excel, if Macros are your shortcuts, think of VBA as the artisan craft behind those shortcuts—enabling you to customize, extend, and ultimately control your Excel environment to do exactly what you need. VBA can be daunting at first glance, but like any language, it becomes more intuitive the more you use it.

Launching into VBA

The first step into VBA doesn't begin with coding, but with understanding how and where to use it. You access VBA through the Developer tab in Excel, which might not be visible by default:

- To enable the 'Developer' tab, click on 'File' > 'Options' > 'Customize Ribbon' and then check the box for 'Developer' in the right pane. This will add the tab to your Excel ribbon.
- In the 'Developer' tab, click on 'Visual Basic' to open the VBA development environment.

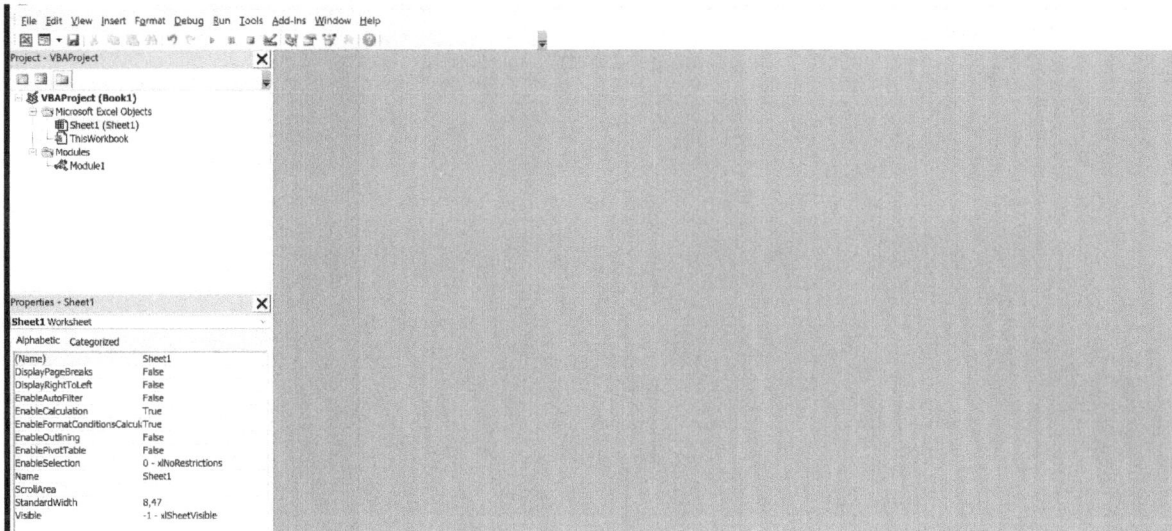

Your First Macro Using VBA

While recording a Macro can automate steps, writing one from scratch launches you into the realm of possibilities. Let's write a simple Macro. Imagine a daily task where you format a report—adjusting column widths and applying text formatting. Here's how you could automate it:

1. **Open the VBA Editor**: In Excel, under the 'Developer' tab, click on 'Visual Basic'.

2. **Insert a Module**: In the VBA editor, right-click on 'VBAProject (YourWorkbookName)' and choose 'Insert' > 'Module'. This is where you'll write your code.

3. **Write Your Macro**: ``` Sub FormatReport() ' Set column widths Columns("A:A").ColumnWidth = 20 Columns("B:B").ColumnWidth = 30 Columns("C:C").ColumnWidth = 40

4. ' Set text format

5. Range("A1:C1").Font.Bold = True

6. Range("A1:C1").Font.Size = 12

7. Range("A1:C1").HorizontalAlignment = xlCenter

End Sub ```

8. **Run Your Macro**: Go back to Excel, under 'Developer' > 'Macros', find 'FormatReport', and run it.

```
Book1 - Module1 (Code)
(General)                                          Macro1
Sub Macro1()
'
' Macro1 Macro
' Macro 1
'
' Keyboard Shortcut: Ctrl+Shift+L
'
End Sub
```

Decoding the Code

The code Sub FormatReport() starts a new subroutine, named 'FormatReport'. A subroutine in VBA is just a series of statements that carry out an action—in this case, formatting a report.

- Columns("X:X").ColumnWidth = Y adjusts the width of columns.
- Range("A1:C1").Font.Bold = True makes the font bold in the specified range.
- Range("A1:C1").HorizontalAlignment = xlCenter aligns the text centrally.

Practical Tips

- **Comment Your Code**: Use comments in VBA by starting with a '. This won't affect the code but will remind you or inform anyone else what a section of the code does.
- **Use Meaningful Names**: Subroutine names like FormatReport make it easier to remember what your code is doing.

Real-World Example

Imagine an annual audit requiring you to format and present multiple datasets across numerous Excel files. Instead of manually adjusting each workbook, a well-written series of VBA scripts could uniformly style all these documents, ensuring that you accomplish in minutes what might have traditionally taken hours.

Embrace Errors as Learning Opportunities

As you begin, you might encounter bugs or errors in your code. Each error is an opportunity to learn. Use the debugging tools in VBA, like setting breakpoints or using "Debug.Print" to understand how your data is being processed.

The VBA Community

Remember, many Excel users have navigated the initial hurdles of learning VBA and have come out the other side more efficient and capable. Online forums, detailed documentation by Microsoft, and community resources like Stack Overflow can be invaluable.

Keep Practicing

Your journey in mastering VBA coding is just beginning. Start with small, manageable projects, and gradually incorporate more complexity as you become comfortable.

By the end of this exploration of basic VBA, you've not only started speaking a powerful new language but also begun shaping Excel to work smarter for you. Each line of code you write is a step towards deeper mastery of Excel automation, unlocking productivity and insights that are uniquely tailored to your needs. Keep the momentum going, and soon, you'll be transforming both your work and your career with every subroutine you craft.

AUTOMATING REPETITIVE TASKS WITH VBA

The art of automating repetitive tasks using VBA in Excel is akin to setting up dominoes just to see them topple in flawless succession, achieving your end-goal with a mesmerizing ease and precision. VBA, or Visual Basic for Applications, is not merely a feature of Excel—it's a powerful programming environment that, when harnessed correctly, can revolutionize the way you manage data, making tedious tasks a thing of the past and elevating your work efficiency to new heights.

Understanding the Need for Automation

Every professional experiences those moments when repetitive tasks feel like a roadblock to productivity. Maybe it's monthly sales reports that need a particular format, or data that must be pulled and consolidated from multiple sources. These tasks, while necessary, consume time that could otherwise be spent on analysis or strategic planning. Enter VBA—a toolkit designed to tackle such challenges through automation.

Setting the Scene for VBA Automation

To begin automating with VBA, you need to appreciate the common tasks suitable for automation:

- Data entry and formatting tasks.
- Regular report generation.
- Repeatedly extracting data from databases and other sources.

Understanding these contexts and recognizing patterns in your tasks is the first crucial step.

Writing Your First Automation Script

To craft a script in VBA that automates tasks, follow these structured steps:

1. **Identify the Task**: Clearly define what you need to automate. A clear task will lead to a clear script.
2. **Open the VBA Editor**: Activate the Developer tab in Excel, click on 'Visual Basic' to open the VBA Editor.
3. **Insert a New Module**: Right-click on 'VBAProject (Your Workbook)' in the Project pane, select 'Insert', and then 'Module'.
4. **Begin Scripting**: Start scripting by defining what your macro will do.

```
``` Sub AutomateReport() Dim ws as Worksheet Set ws = ThisWorkbook.Sheets("Sales")
' Example: Clear Previous Data
ws.Range("A2:D500").ClearContents


' Example: Insert Data
ws.Range("A2").Value = "New Data"


' Example: Format Report
With ws.Range("A1:D1")
    .Font.Bold = True
    .Font.Color = RGB(255, 255, 255)
    .Interior.Color = RGB(0, 0, 0)
End With
End Sub ```
```
```

Breaking Down the Script

This simple script: - Defines a worksheet object for manipulation.

- Clears previous data.

- Enters new data.

- Applies specific formatting to the header row.

Executing and Testing

After scripting:

- Run the Macro by pressing 'F5' in the VBA editor or via 'Macros' in the Excel interface.

- Evaluate the results. Check if the data appears as intended and whether the format aligns with your requirements.

Enhancing Productivity with Advanced VBA

As you grow more comfortable, you might integrate more complex logic like loops for handling large data sets, or conditions that apply changes based on specific criteria: vba For Each cell In ws.Range("A2:A500") If cell.Value > 1000 Then cell.Interior.Color = RGB(255, 0, 0) End If Next cell This code snippet scans each cell in the designated range and changes the background to red where the values exceed 1000, thereby quickly highlighting significant figures.

Real-World Application

Imagine a scenario: a financial analyst automating the extraction and consolidation of financial reports from various departments. VBA scripts can streamline data aggregation, apply necessary financial calculations, and format the final report for easier decision-making, turning what used to be hours of work into mere minutes.

Tips for Success

- **Clarify Your Goals**: Understand what you need from your macro. A well-defined goal ensures a targeted script.

- **Validate Regularly**: Regularly test pieces of your code to avoid surprises at the end.

- **Document Your Code**: Use comments generously to explain the purpose of parts of your script, aiding future adjustments or expansions by you or colleagues.

The Promise of Automation

With these skills at your disposal, it's possible to transform your interaction with Excel. No longer bound by manual constraints, your work can shift towards strategic, value-added activities. The leap from performing repetitive tasks to automating them with VBA not only enhances productivity, but also expands your analytical capabilities, turning mundane data management into a streamlined, efficient process that solidifies your role as a proficient and forward-thinking professional.

DEBUGGING AND TROUBLESHOOTING MACROS

Navigating the realm of Excel macros involves more than just crafting effective automation scripts; it also requires the ability to identify and rectify errors—a process known colloquially as debugging. Mastering debugging and troubleshooting is as crucial as knowing how to write the macros in the first place, because it ensures your automation tools function seamlessly and efficiently.

Understanding the Nature of Bugs in Macros

In the world of Excel VBA, 'bugs' are errors or flaws in your code that cause the macro to behave unexpectedly or halt entirely. These can range from simple typos to more complex logical errors. Debugging, then, is the detective work of coding; it's about tracking down the culprit(s) and rectifying them.

Common Sources of Bugs

Most bugs in macros fall into one of several categories:

- **Syntax errors**: These are mistakes in the code's language, like typos or incorrect command usage, which are usually caught by the VBA editor itself.
- **Runtime errors**: These occur when the VBA code attempts to perform an illegal operation, such as dividing by zero or attempting to access a resource that isn't available.
- **Logical errors**: Perhaps the trickiest to catch, these are errors where the code doesn't produce an error message but still doesn't work as intended due to flawed logic.

Step-by-Step Debugging Techniques

1. **Using the VBA Editor Tools**

    o   **Breakpoints**: A breakpoint can be set by clicking in the margin next to a line of code. This tells VBA to pause execution at that point, letting you examine the current state of the program.

    o   **Step Through Execution**: Use the F8 key to step through your code line by line. This allows you to observe the changes in variable values and the flow of execution in real-time.

2. **Watching Variables**:

    o   The 'Watch' window in VBA lets you monitor the values of selected variables as your code executes. This is particularly helpful for spotting unexpected changes that may be causing issues.

3. **Immediate Window**:

    o   Use the Immediate Window for quick tests and queries about the current state of your program. You can execute lines of code here to see how they affect your macro without needing to run the macro itself.

Handling Specific Common Errors

*   **Error Handlers**: Incorporate error handling in your macros with On Error GoTo [label] statements. These direct your macro to proceed to a label line if an error occurs, bypassing the line that caused the error and allowing you to handle it gracefully. vba Sub SampleMacro() On Error GoTo ErrorHandler ' Code that might cause an error Exit Sub ErrorHandler: MsgBox "An error occurred" End Sub

*   **Compile Often**: Use the 'Compile VBAProject' under the 'Debug' menu to check your code for errors periodically during the writing process. This will catch syntax and some logical errors before you even try to run your macro.

*   **Clear Object References**: Objects like worksheets or ranges should be set to Nothing once you're done using them. This helps prevent issues related to lingering references that might not be valid in subsequent runs of your macro.

Practical Tips for Efficient Debugging

- **Keep your code tidy**: Use indentations and follow a consistent coding style. Well-organized code is much easier to debug because it's easier to follow logically.

- **Document your code**: Use comments generously to explain sections of code, especially where the logic isn't immediately obvious. This can be a lifesaver when you're trying to figure out why a particular section isn't working as expected.

- **Divide and Conquer**: If a particular macro is causing trouble, try to isolate which part of the code is problematic by testing small sections at a time.

Real-World Example

Consider a scenario where an Excel macro designed to calculate monthly expenses keeps crashing. By strategically placing breakpoints and using the Immediate Window to monitor variable values, you might discover that the macro attempts to divide by zero when processing a day with no recorded expenses. Handling this by adding a simple If statement to check for zero before division can resolve the issue promptly.

The Continuous Learning Curve

Debugging is as much a part of the VBA journey as writing the code itself. With each bug you encounter and fix, your understanding of both your code and VBA grows deeper. Each challenge becomes an opportunity to refine your approach to both coding and problem-solving within the Excel environment.

As you develop your debugging skills, remember that the goal is always clear: to ensure your macros run as efficiently and effectively as possible, minimizing downtime and maximizing your productivity. Welcome these challenges as steps towards becoming a seasoned Excel VBA programmer, capable of navigating and resolving whatever issues arise.

CHAPTER 9: BUSINESS & FINANCIAL APPLICATIONS

Welcome to the dynamic world of business and financial applications in Excel, where you're not just learning a tool but mastering a skill that can significantly elevate your professional landscape. Imagine being able to predict the financial health of your project with a few inputs or strategizing your budget in a way that not only saves money but also sources it more effectively. That's the power of Excel in business and finance which we're going to delve into today.

Throughout this journey, we have unlocked various facets of Excel, tackling everything from foundational data handling to complex automation. Today, we reach the pinnacle of practical application, as Excel becomes more than software—it transforms into your financial advisor, your business strategist.

Let's start with budgeting and forecasting. These are not just tasks but necessary skills for steering projects and businesses towards profitability and growth. With Excel, you can turn historical data into a predictive tool that forecasts trends and prepares you for future financial needs. The art of creating accurate forecasts might seem complex, but it is quite attainable when you peel back the layers of data and look at it through the lens of logical and functional Excel formulas.

Next up, we will navigate the realms of project management. Excel allows you to build precise Gantt charts and set clear milestones, ensuring project timelines are met with precision. Remember, a well-laid plan in Excel is half the battle won. From allocating resources effectively to tracking ongoing progress, these tools are indispensable.

As we round up, we'll explore inventory management and expense tracking—where every cent counts. Using Excel to maintain meticulous records not only helps in keeping the finances tight but also in conducting spontaneous audits that can save you from a plethora of troubles down the line.

By the end of this chapter, Excel will no longer just be a program you use; it will be an integral part of how you strategize, analyze, and succeed in your business endeavors. Let's embark on this final leg of our Excel adventure, where numbers meet strategy, and plans meet profitability.

EXCEL FOR BUDGETING AND FORECASTING

In the landscape of business, the ability to plan financially and forecast accurately is akin to possessing a crystal ball. As we dive deeper into Excel's capabilities for budgeting and forecasting, envision yourself navigating the complexities of financial data with the ease of an expert sailor charting familiar waters. Our goal here is to transform Excel from a mere tool to your trusted financial advisor.

Starting with Budgeting

Every robust business practice begins with the formulation of a clear, precise budget. In Excel, this starts with setting up your budgeting template, which effectively organizes incoming data for analysis.

1. **Create Your Template**: Begin by opening a new Excel workbook. Label the first column with the months of the year or specific periods relevant to your budgeting needs. Following columns should represent different categories of income and expenses. This setup forms the backbone of your budget, giving you a clear overview of financial inflows and outflows.

2. **Input Historical Data**: If you have past financial data, input this into your corresponding categories. This historical data will be invaluable as you project future budgets.

3. **Formulate Projections**: Using Excel's various functions, you can calculate projected values for different categories. Use simple formulas like =SUM() for totals or =AVERAGE() for expected income or expenses based on past trends. This step transitions you from mere data entry to analytical forecasting.

4. **Adjust for Seasonality**: Businesses often see financial fluctuations due to seasonal changes. Excel's capabilities allow you to adjust your budget projections to account for these variations. Using conditional formatting, highlight months where you anticipate increases or decreases in budget categories, providing visual cues for further analysis.

5. **Continuous Updates**: As actual data comes in, update your budget. This practice not only keeps your projections realistic but also leverages Excel's power to recalibrate data based on new inputs.

Advancing to Forecasting

With your budget set, forecasting future financial health becomes your next navigational target. Forecasting, while inherently speculative, can be made more accurate with Excel's powerful analytical tools.

1. **Begin with Baselines**: Your budget data now becomes your base for forecasting. Ensure your baseline figures are as accurate and detailed as possible to improve the quality of your forecasts.

2. **Use Excel Forecasting Functions**: Leverage functions like FORECAST.LINEAR to predict a future point along a linear trend line. For example, forecast next year's sales based on current year trends. This function takes into account seasonality, offering a more refined prediction.

3. **Scenario Analysis**: via Excel's What-If analysis tools such as Data Tables, Scenarios, and Goal Seek, simulate different financial scenarios. For instance, what if an unexpected expense increases? Or, what impact will a 10% sales increase have on your bottom line? These tools allow you to prepare multiple future outcomes, helping mitigate risks.

4. **Dynamic Charts for Visualization**: Transform your data into dynamic charts—like line graphs or bar charts—which update as you input new data. This visualization not only aids in understanding trends over time but also helps in presenting data to stakeholders succinctly.

5. **Regular Revisions**: Just as with budgeting, revisiting your forecasts regularly is crucial. As new data becomes available or as market conditions change, adjust your forecasts. This iterative process keeps your forecasts realistic and actionable.

Practical Tips for Precision

While the function of Excel for budgeting and forecasting is robust, precision is key.

- **Consistency in Data Entry**: Always format dates and financial figures uniformly to avoid discrepancies that can skew results.
- **Leverage Excel Add-Ins**: For advanced budgeting and forecasting, consider Excel add-ins like Solver or Analysis ToolPak, which provide additional statistical and engineering analysis capabilities.
- **Automate Where Possible**: Use macros to automate repetitive tasks like monthly calculations and data formatting, saving you time and reducing the potential for errors.

Real-World Applications

Consider the scenario of a small business looking to expand. Applying these techniques, the owner can forecast additional costs and predict revenues from expansion, hence making informed decisions about whether expansion is financially viable.

By mastering budgeting and forecasting in Excel, you're not just staying afloat in the vast sea of business operations—you are confidently steering your ship towards your desired financial goals. Remember, each step in Excel adds a layer of sophistication to your financial strategies, turning raw data into a goldmine of actionable insights. Through this structured approach, Excel does more than just compute; it illuminates the path to financial wisdom and business acumen.

PROJECT MANAGEMENT WITH EXCEL (GANTT CHARTS, MILESTONES)

The management of projects is akin to conducting a meticulously orchestrated symphony. Each element must be in perfect sync, and the conductor—much like a project manager—must have visibility into every section of the orchestra. Excel, with its robust capabilities for Gantt charts and tracking milestones, proves an invaluable tool for this very purpose.

Transforming Excel into Your Project Management Hub

Excel isn't just about crunching numbers; it's a versatile tool that can be transformed into a powerful project management solution. By leveraging Gantt charts and setting precise milestones, project managers can gain unparalleled insights into project timelines, resource allocation, and progress tracking.

Crafting a Gantt Chart from Scratch

A Gantt chart in Excel provides a visual timeline for project schedules, helping you visualize project tasks and their respective durations.

1. **Setting Up Your Spreadsheet**: Start by listing all the tasks involved in your project in the first column. Next to your tasks, input the task's start date, the duration, and the end date in separate columns.

2. **Creating a Timeline**: Utilize the bar chart feature in Excel to transform your data into a visual timeline. Convert the 'Start Date' to your primary horizontal axis and task durations to data bars stretching across a timeline. This visualization immediately offers insights into overlapping tasks and project flow.

3. **Customizing Your Gantt Chart**: Add colors to differentiate between tasks, departments, or phases. Utilize conditional formatting to highlight critical paths or overdue tasks. This level of customization not only makes your Gantt chart easier to read but also turns it into an effective communication tool.

Incorporating Milestones

Milestones are significant goals or checkpoints used to gauge the progress of a project. Excel allows you to seamlessly integrate these into your Gantt chart.

1. **Identifying Milestones**: Define clear, measurable milestones that signify major achievements or phases in the project. Examples include the completion of the foundational phase, finalizing a major deliverable, or achieving regulatory approval.

2. **Adding Milestones to Your Chart**: In Excel, represent milestones as distinct markers on your Gantt chart, perhaps using a different shape or color. Position them on the corresponding completion dates along the timeline to provide a snapshot view of critical dates throughout the project.

Progress Tracking and Updates

The dynamic nature of projects necessitates regular updates to your Gantt chart and milestones.

1. **Regular Monitoring**: Set regular intervals (daily, weekly, monthly) to update the Gantt chart. Adjust the durations, change colors for completed tasks, or shift milestones as needed based on real-time project developments.

2. **Linking Task Dependencies**: In larger projects, tasks often depend on the completion of others. Excel allows you to link tasks visually and logically, helping to manage dependencies and adjust timelines dynamically.

3. **Automation Features**: Utilize Excel formulas to automatically update task durations and end dates based on dependencies. This reduces manual adjustments and helps maintain an accurate project timeline.

Practical Tips for Effective Management

- **Resource Allocation**: Use a separate section of your Gantt chart to allocate resources. This helps you keep tabs on who is doing what, ensuring that no single team member is overburdened.

- **Risk Management**: Integrate risk assessment directly beside related tasks on your Gantt chart. This could be as simple as a risk score or a colored indicator showing the risk level.

- **Communication**: Regularly share your updated Gantt chart with stakeholders. This keeps everyone informed and aligned on project progress and expectations.

Real-World Application

Imagine a software development project. By using a Gantt chart, the project manager visualizes the entire development cycle—from initial planning, through coding, testing, to final deployment. As the project progresses, each stage is updated in the chart, providing a clear picture of early or delayed phases, thereby allowing timely decisions like resource reallocation or schedule adjustments.

Using Excel for project management is about more than just tracking; it's about gaining a strategic view of your projects, empowering you to manage more effectively and react swiftly to changing dynamics. Through meticulous planning, continuous adaptation, and effective communication, Excel's tools transform the complex task of project management into a more manageable and visually engaging experience. With every project phase and milestone laid out clearly, you stand ready to guide your team toward timely and successful project completions.

INVENTORY AND EXPENSE TRACKING

In the bustling world of business, keeping a vigilant eye on inventory levels and tracking expenses is not just good practice—it's a critical component of financial health and operational efficiency. Excel, your trusty digital tool, is about to become your most reliable partner in this essential task. Imagine transforming the daunting task of inventory and expense management into a streamlined, error-minimized process, all residing within the familiar grids of an Excel spreadsheet.

Mastering Inventory Management

The heart of good inventory management in Excel lies in creating a system that is both easy to update and comprehensive enough to give you a full snapshot of your stock at any given time.

Setting Up Your Inventory Spreadsheet

Start by opening a new Excel workbook dedicated to your inventory. Your initial setup should include columns for item names, SKU numbers, unit price, quantity in stock, reorder level, and categories if needed.

- **Item Names and SKU Numbers**: Each item in your inventory should have a unique identifier or SKU number which helps in tracking and reduces errors.
- **Unit Price and Quantity in Stock**: These are critical for financial assessments. Knowing your stock levels in real-time helps in making informed purchasing decisions.
- **Reorder Level**: Set up conditional formatting to highlight items that fall below a certain threshold, prompting timely reordering to avoid stock-outs.

Regularly Update Inventory Data

As stock levels change with new shipments arriving and items being sold or used, regular updates are crucial. Implement a routine, whether daily or weekly, to adjust the quantities. This practice minimizes discrepancies and maintains the integrity of your inventory management system.

Streamlining Expense Tracking

Tracking expenses meticulously not only helps in maintaining budgets but also provides insights into cost-saving areas. With Excel, you can set up an expense tracker that captures every financial outflow with precision and context.

Creating an Expense Tracker

Set up a new workbook or a separate sheet in your inventory workbook for expenses. Your primary columns will include date, expense category, amount, vendor, and payment status.

- **Date and Expense Category**: These help in organizing expenses over time and by type, making it easier to review and analyze spending patterns.
- **Amount and Vendor**: Keeping track of how much is spent and whom it's paid to aids in financial transparency and accountability.
- **Payment Status**: Track which expenses have been paid, are due, or are overdue. Use conditional formatting to highlight overdue payments.

Integrating Inventory and Expense Systems

Once your systems for tracking inventory and expenses are operational, integrating these can lead to deeper insights and efficiencies.

- **Linking Expenses to Inventory**: For businesses that sell products, linking procurement expenses back to specific inventory items can provide exact cost evaluations for each product.
- **Dashboard Creation**: Use Excel's capabilities to create a dashboard that combines key metrics from both inventory and expenses. This could include total inventory valuation, most recent expenditures, and low stock alerts.

Analytical Insights and Reporting

Use Excel's built-in functions like pivot tables and charts to extract actionable insights from your inventory and expense data. Regular analysis can identify trends, such as seasonal increases in inventory levels or significant shifts in expense categories.

- **Pivot Tables**: Summarize large data sets to see total expenses per category or per vendor. Similarly, analyze inventory turnover rates or identify items with frequent stock-outs.
- **Charts and Graphs**: Visually represent data, such as monthly expenses over time or comparison charts showing projected versus actual expenses.

Automation for Efficiency

Consider automating repetitive tasks with Excel's macros or implementing formulas that simplify calculations, such as totaling monthly expenses or automatically updating inventory levels.

- **Macros**: These can automate data entry tasks, like copying and pasting data between sheets, or complex calculations that need to be repeated regularly.
- **Formulas**: Use formulas like VLOOKUP to pull information from one sheet to another automatically, ensuring that all parts of your Excel system are consistently updated.

Practical Tips and Real-World Application

Maintain a clean and organized layout to make navigation easier. Keeping your sheets clearly labeled and free of clutter reduces errors and enhances usability. Regular backups of your Excel files can prevent data loss.

Consider the scenario where a small retailer leverages Excel to manage inventory across multiple store locations. By setting up interconnected sheets that feed into a centralized system, management can quickly see which items are performing best, which stores require more stock, and monitor expenses tied to each location efficiently.

Through careful setup, diligent updates, and integration of systems, Excel becomes more than just a software application—it stands as your central command for inventory and expense management, driving efficiency and providing critical insights that support strategic business decisions.

DATA CLEANING AND TRANSFORMATION TECHNIQUES

In the realm of data-driven decision-making, the purity and precision of your data are paramount. Imagine launching a mission to Mars, but your navigation charts are filled with inaccuracies. Even minor errors could lead disastrously off course. This same principle applies to the world of business analytics within Excel. Data cleaning and transformation aren't just preparatory steps; they are critical missions ensuring that every subsequent decision based on your data is informed and accurate.

The Art of Data Cleaning

Data cleaning involves removing or correcting data that is incorrect, incomplete, duplicated, or improperly formatted. This process is crucial because even the smallest error can lead to skewed results and faulty business decisions.

Identifying and Removing Duplicates

Duplicates can often occur during data collection or integration from multiple sources. Excel offers a straightforward feature for identifying and removing duplicated entries. Utilizing the 'Remove Duplicates' button under the Data tab effectively cleans your dataset, ensuring that each entry is unique and that your analysis is precise.

Correcting Inconsistencies

Inconsistent data often appears in the form of varying formats or typographical errors. For instance, the same city name might be entered as "New York," "new york," or "NY." Using the 'Text to Columns' feature can help standardize this data. Further refinement can be achieved by applying Excel's 'Find and Replace' functionality, which assists in correcting frequent misspellings or alternate spellings quickly.

Handling Missing Values

Missing data can skew analysis and lead to invalid conclusions. Options to handle missing values include:

- Removing the row entirely, which is advisable only if the missing data constitutes a small fraction of your dataset.
- Inputting a substitute value, like the average or median of that column, which can be done using Excel's formula capabilities such as =AVERAGE(range) or =MEDIAN(range).
- Using predictive techniques to fill in missing values, though this typically requires more advanced statistical software integrated with Excel.

Transforming Data for Analysis

Once your data is cleaned, transforming it into a usable format for analysis is the next crucial phase. This involves rearranging or aggregating data to better suit analytical models or report formats.

Normalizing Data

Data normalization involves adjusting values measured on different scales to a notionally common scale, often required in statistical or data science applications. Excel does not have a built-in function for this but can be accomplished using formulae like (cell - MIN(range)) / (MAX(range) - MIN(range)).

Pivot Tables for Aggregation

Pivot tables are incredibly powerful tools in Excel for summarizing, analyzing, exploring, and presenting data. They allow you to extract the significance from a large, detailed data set by reorganizing and summarizing selected columns and rows of data. Whether it's summing up expenses by category, averaging sales by region, or counting distinct products sold, Pivot tables make it quick and easy.

Data Type Conversion

Often, data imported from other sources into Excel might not be in the format you need. For example, dates might be represented as text strings. Excel's TEXT TO COLUMNS wizard, along with custom formatting features, allows for the conversion of text to date formats, or integers to strings, ensuring that data types are consistent for analysis.

Regular Maintenance and Auditing

Regularly scheduled data cleaning and transformation should not be an afterthought but a fundamental part of your data management strategy. Setting up periodic reviews of your datasets ensures maintenance of data integrity and relevance, adapting as new data comes in or as business needs evolve.

Creating a Data Audit Trail

Maintain documentation of how data is collected, cleaned, transformed, and analyzed. This practice not only ensures transparency but also makes it easier to trace back and understand the steps taken should discrepancies arise later on.

Utilizing Excel Add-Ins

For advanced data cleaning and transformation tasks, consider utilizing Excel add-ins like Power Query. These tools offer powerful ways to automate data ingestion, cleaning, and preparation processes, making them repeatable and efficient.

Real-World Application: Marketing Campaign Analysis

Consider a marketing analyst at an e-commerce company tasked with evaluating the effectiveness of various marketing campaigns. The raw data from different platforms contains inconsistencies in campaign names and formats, along with missing values in the budget spent.

After cleaning the data in Excel—removing duplicates, standardizing names, and estimating missing budget entries—the analyst uses pivot tables to summarize total expenditure and revenue by campaign type, revealing the ROI for each campaign.

The journey through data cleaning and transformation is a meticulous yet profoundly rewarding pathway. It empowers you to forge your analytical endeavors on robust, reliable ground, ensuring that every insight extracted and every decision made is built on the bedrock of clean, clear, and concise data. With these techniques, your Excel spreadsheets won't just be data repositories; they'll transform into beacons of strategic intelligence, guiding your business decisions with the confidence that only comes from quality data.

CHAPTER 10: COLLABORATION, SECURITY, AND POWER FEATURES

Welcome to the pivotal chapter that ties together not just numbers and charts, but people and processes. As we segue into the sophisticated layers of Excel, understand that your journey up until now has prepared you to deploy Excel's capabilities not just on your computer, but in an interconnected workspace.

Imagine you're at a bustling coffee shop, fingers poised over the laptop, collaborating in real-time with a team situated across the globe. Excel isn't just about solitary number-crunching; it's your collaborative partner that connects your insights with those of your colleagues through powerful, shareable dashboards and seamless data integration.

Yet, as we dive deeper into sharing and collaboration, the whispers of data breaches and security flaws might be nibbling at the edges of your mind. Here, we address these not as looming threats, but as challenges that can be tamed with the right Excel tools. Locking cells, protecting sensitive formulas, and managing access only scratches the surface of securing your Excel environment.

We often hear about the digital transformation in business but think about how Excel facilitates this by integrating with tools like Power BI to bring dynamic data visualization that drives decisions with the precision of a Swiss watch. You're not just learning Excel; you're learning to maneuver the cutting edge of business intelligence tools.

And let's not forget the power under the hood – Power Query and Power Pivot transform massive amounts of data not into intimidating jumbles, but into clear, actionable insights. This isn't just about making your work easier; it's about amplifying your impact on your organization, ensuring that every pivot table, every data model brings you closer to not just goals, but breakthroughs.

So, as we turn the page to this exploration, remember that you're arming yourself not just with knowledge, but with collaboration prowess, fortified security measures, and integration skills that will make you indispensable in this digital age. Let's master these advanced features, not just to use Excel, but to excel in transforming data into decisions.

PROTECTING AND SECURING WORKBOOKS (PASSWORD PROTECTION, LOCKING CELLS)

In the realm of Excel use, ensuring data security is akin to safeguarding your digital treasure chest. Let's delve into the nuances of protecting and securing your precious workbooks. Envision someone accidentally—or maliciously—tampering with your comprehensive financial models or sensitive data projections. The results could range from disruptive to disastrous. Excel, understanding the stakes, provides a robust package of security features that are your loyal gatekeepers.

Starting with the simplest yet most pivotal security measure, Excel allows you to **password-protect your workbook**. Implementing this is straightforward, yet it creates a formidable barrier against unauthorized access. When you try to open a password-protected workbook, Excel requires you to enter the password you've set up—no correct password, no entry.

To enable this protection, open your file and access the 'File' tab. Click on 'Info' and then select 'Protect Workbook'. Here, you'll find the option to 'Encrypt with Password'. A dialog box will appear prompting you to enter your password. Choose a strong password—a combination of letters, numbers, and symbols is recommended—and confirm it by entering it a second time. Now, every time the workbook is opened, Excel will require this password.

However, it's crucial to note that maintaining the confidentiality of your password is as integral as setting it. Excel's password encryption is robust, but no security measure can withstand compromised confidentiality.

Next, consider a scenario where you find it necessary to allow access to the entire workbook but need to restrict modifications to specific cells. Excel equips you with the ability to **lock cells**. By default, all cells in an Excel sheet are locked, but this effect only comes into play when you protect the worksheet. Here's how you do it: Start by selecting the cells or range you want to leave unlocked. Right-click and choose 'Format Cells', then navigate to the 'Protection' tab. You'll see 'Locked' checked by default; uncheck it for these cells.

Once you've designated the unlocked cells, safeguard your worksheet. Go to the 'Review' tab, click on 'Protect Sheet', and then decide what actions you want users to be able to perform—like formatting cells, sorting data, or filtering tables. Set a password for unprotecting the worksheet here as well.

Importantly, should you ever need to edit locked cells, you'll return to the 'Review' tab and select 'Unprotect Sheet', then enter the previously set password. You can now make your modifications and re-protect the sheet afterward.

But what if your workbook is more than just a series of spreadsheets? What if it includes VBA macros that automate significant tasks within your data sets? Excel hasn't left this stone unturned. Protecting your VBA code is as essential as securing your data cells.

To secure your macros, access the VBA editor by pressing 'ALT + F11'. Right-click on VBAProject in the left pane, select 'VBAProject Properties,' and navigate to the 'Protection' tab. Here, check 'Lock project for viewing' and set a password. Just like with workbook protection, this password should be noted securely, as losing it can lock you out of your own code indefinitely.

Each protection feature serves its purpose, from safeguarding sensitive financial forecasts to keeping your strategic pivots confidential. But, balance is key.

Overprotecting can become an operational hindrance. Select your security settings based on the sensitivity of the workbook's contents and the trust level within your team.

Remember, while Excel features robust tools to protect and secure your data, they are only effective if implemented wisely. Regularly review who has access to your data and adjust protections as necessary. Excel is a powerful ally in data security, guarding your information from unwarranted access while enabling the smooth, selective flow of operations where needed. Each step, from setting a simple password to locking crucial cells, is a building block towards safeguarding your digital assets, letting you focus on what you do best: analyzing data and deriving valuable insights.

Thus, taking these steps not only enhances security but also fosters a disciplined approach to data management—turning potential vulnerabilities into fortified strengths.

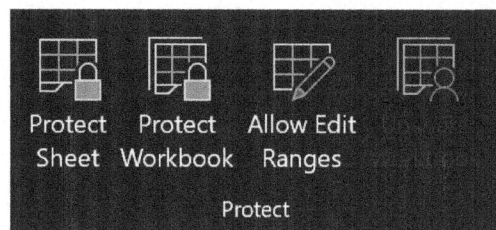

COLLABORATION FEATURES: TRACK CHANGES, COMMENTS, AND SHARED WORKBOOKS

In the bustling world of business and data management, Excel emerges not just as a tool for individual data manipulation, but as a robust platform for team collaboration. Your workbook can transform from a static table of information to a dynamic canvas where ideas, revisions, and updates fluidly blend together through Excel's collaboration tools. Let's explore these essential mechanisms—Track Changes, Comments, and Shared Workbooks—which evolve your spreadsheet into an interactive portal, connecting minds and fostering teamwork effectively.

When several hands are stirring the pot, it's vital to know who added what ingredient. Track Changes in Excel acts as your discrete observer, quietly noting every modification made by team members. This feature becomes indispensable for ensuring transparency and accountability in collaborative environments. To enable Track Changes, navigate to the 'Review' tab and select 'Track Changes'. Here, you can opt to 'Highlight Changes', and configure settings to track changes made by everyone, or just specific colleagues. You'll also decide whether to track changes on the fly or to list them on a separate sheet. Each change will then be marked, showing who made it and when, resembling a silent audit trail of your datasheet's evolution.

Moving beyond tracking to active dialogue, Comments in Excel serve as your team's conversation hub. Imagine each cell in your spreadsheet as a meeting room. Comments allow team members to leave notes, raise questions, or provide insights directly linked to specific data points. Click on a cell, and go to 'New Comment' under the 'Review' tab. Comments can be as simple as "Check these figures", or can spark richer discussions about the data's implications.

In newer versions of Excel, comments have evolved into threaded discussions, allowing multiple colleagues to engage in back-and-forths as one would in a digital workplace chatroom.

Now, to harness the full potential of these tools, consider the environment of Shared Workbooks, which allow multiple users to work on the same file simultaneously. This feature democratizes data handling, letting all designated users access and modify the workbook in real-time or asynchronously. To turn this on, head to the 'Review' tab, and from 'Share Workbook', check the box that allows multiple users to edit the workbook at the same time. Sharing setups can be fine-tuned based on network locations, and who needs what level of access, ensuring a controlled yet flexible collaborative environment.

Utilizing these features effectively does require a blend of technological savvy and nuanced management skills. For instance, with Track Changes, while it's beneficial to monitor edits, too many changes tracked over long periods can clutter your workbook, making it less efficient. Regularly review and accept/reject changes to maintain clarity. Similarly, while comments are great for communication, unresolved threads can become confusing. Make it a practice within your team to resolve comments once the discussed tasks are completed, keeping the workbook clean and focused.

Another nuanced tip: when using Shared Workbooks, be aware of the potential for conflicts when two users try to modify the same cell simultaneously. Excel handles this by prompting users when conflicts arise, offering options to choose between changes. Promoting etiquette and coordination during collaborative sessions can minimize such conflicts and enhance smooth collaborative workflows.

And as we incorporate these tools into our daily routines, integrating them with other elements of our digital infrastructure can unlock even more potential. Comments and track changes could feed into broader project management tools, ensuring that changes to data are reflected in project timelines and task assignments. Similarly, data from shared workbooks can be linked to real-time dashboards, providing updated insights to stakeholders across the organization.

As we close the discussion on enhancing teamwork through Excel, remember that successful collaboration isn't just about using the right tools; it's also about fostering a culture of openness, respect, and mutual understanding.

By effectively leveraging features like Track Changes, Comments, and Shared Workbooks, you equip your team with the means not only to work together but to think, innovate, and succeed together. These tools, when used thoughtfully, do not just make your workflows easier; they make your organizational knowledge richer and more accessible, paving the way for informed decisions and cohesive strategies.

Excel, thus, is more than a spreadsheet application—it's a catalyst for collective achievement in the modern data-driven workspace.

INTEGRATING EXCEL WITH POWER BI AND AI-DRIVEN ANALYTICS

In today's fast-paced business environment, mastering Excel is just the beginning. The true power lies in how seamlessly it integrates with advanced analytics platforms, such as Power BI and AI-driven analytics tools, transforming raw data into strategic insights. It's like watching a grainy black-and-white photo turn into a dynamic 3D movie—suddenly, everything is clearer, more impactful, and infinitely more useful.

Firstly, let's explore the integration between Excel and Power BI. Think of Excel as your digital notebook where you gather, organize, and preliminarily analyze your data. Power BI, on the other hand, is like a high-powered magnifying glass that can see not just the surface details but also the intricate patterns hidden within the data. By connecting Excel to Power BI, your spreadsheets blossom into fully interactive reports and dashboards, providing deeper insights and real-time updates.

To bridge Excel and Power BI, you start simply by importing your Excel datasets into Power BI. Once there, you can harness Power BI's robust analytical tools to create comprehensive visualizations. This integration allows users to drill down into specifics with just a few clicks, reading between the lines of data in ways that static tables can't manage. The beauty of this setup is the fluidity with which data updates: changes made in your Excel spreadsheet can reflect immediately in Power BI, ensuring that your insights are always based on the latest data.

But the journey doesn't end at high-power analytics. Enter the realm of AI-driven analytics. Here's where Excel acts not just as a source of data but as a participant in a broader analytical ecosystem. With Excel connected to AI tools, you can perform complex predictive analytics, use natural language processing to generate intuitive queries, or create models that forecast trends based on vast data sets that stretch beyond what one might diligently crunch on a spreadsheet.

For instance, consider integrating Excel with an AI platform like Azure Machine Learning. This tool allows users to build, train, and deploy machine learning models that can enhance the quality of business decisions. By feeding data from Excel directly into these models, you can automate the task of making sense of large volumes of information, from predicting customer behavior to optimizing operational processes.

What makes this integration particularly compelling is the ease with which non-data scientists can partake in AI-driven analytics.

Tools have evolved to be more user-friendly, often requiring no more than a basic understanding of the datasets and a clear idea of what you need the AI to analyze. With a few clicks, data from Excel can be set to feed into AI models that return their predictions directly back into your spreadsheet or an interactive Power BI dashboard.

Moreover, when talking about automating with AI, it's not just about heavy statistical computations or futuristic algorithms. Simpler, everyday tasks like data cleansing and sorting, which traditionally consume hours of manual work, can be automated. AI can learn to recognize patterns and errors, suggesting corrections automatically, thereby saving time and reducing the chance for human error.

Yet, with great power comes great responsibility. Integrating AI into your Excel environment must be managed with an understanding of the limitations and ethical implications of AI. Ensuring data privacy, understanding model bias, and maintaining transparency in how decisions are automated are integral parts of leveraging AI responsibly.

In this interconnected setup, Excel acts as the gateway through which data moves seamlessly from the familiar grid of cells to sophisticated analytical models, providing actionable insights that are both predictive and reactive. Whether it's forecasting sales, analyzing market trends, or automating routine reports, the integration of Excel with Power BI and AI-driven tools represents a significant leap towards advanced data-driven decision-making.

Embracing these tools will not just enhance your professional capabilities but will also position you at the forefront of technological innovation in data analysis. With each step of this integration, your role evolves from data entry and analysis to strategic decision-making, supported by cutting-edge tools that harness the collective power of Excel, Power BI, and artificial intelligence. This journey demonstrates the evolution from simple spreadsheet management to comprehensive business intelligence handling, marking a milestone in any professional's career path.

MASTERING POWER QUERY AND POWER PIVOT FOR ADVANCED DATA ANALYSIS

In the rich tapestry of Excel functionalities, Power Query and Power Pivot hold a special place. They are not merely features—they are gateways to advanced data analysis, simplifying what previously was complex and time-consuming.

These powerful tools empower you to handle large datasets with more agility and insight than ever before, turning raw numbers into strategic information.

Imagine Power Query as your steadfast assistant, streamlining the process of collecting and transforming data. With it, you can effortlessly import, cleanse, and consolidate data from various sources—be it databases, spreadsheets, or even web pages.

But Power Query's true brilliance shines in how it allows you to automate these tasks. Once you set up a query, it can be refreshed with new data adhering to the same transformations and conditions, saving you from repetitive manual updates.

On the other hand, Power Pivot extends this capability further by enhancing the analysis and modeling segments. It allows you to create sophisticated data models within Excel, use advanced DAX (Data Analysis Expressions) formulas, and craft intricate pivot tables and charts that slice your data across multiple dimensions effortlessly. It's as if you've been given a sharper lens to examine the intricacies of your data landscape.

Let's illustrate with a common scenario: you manage sales data from multiple regions, each stored in separate files or databases. With Power Query, you can pull all this data into Excel, automatically removing duplicates, filtering out incomplete records, and converting data types appropriately. You then seamlessly transition this cleaned dataset into Power Pivot, where you relate different tables (like sales and inventory), define calculated columns or measures using DAX, such as profit margins, and analyze trends over time or across categories.

Furthermore, consider the interaction between these tools and your broader workflow. As you refine your model in Power Pivot, any updates or additions to your dataset managed in Power Query are reflected automatically, ensuring your analysis always rests on the most current data. This integration not only sharpens your insights but also enhances collaborative efforts as your team can work on the most updated, accurate datasets.

One of the pivotal benefits here is how approachable these tools make the data handling process. Power Query's intuitive interface lets you manipulate data with simple, menu-driven options. Even those new to data work can establish queries and manage complex data sources without writing a single line of code. Meanwhile, Power Pivot's use of DAX might initially seem daunting due to its formula-driven approach. Yet, many find these formulas syntactically similar to Excel's native formulas, easing the learning curve.

This ease of use does not sacrifice depth; both tools offer profound depth for those who wish to dive deeper. For example, Power Query's advanced editor lets seasoned users manually tweak scripts for precise control over data transformations.

Concurrently, Power Pivot's ability to handle and analyze data models with millions of rows of data, far surpassing Excel's traditional row limits, allows analysts to undertake extensive, complex projects that were previously the domain of specialized statistical software.

To make the most of these tools, it's essential to recognize the scenarios they are best suited for. Power Query is your first choice for automating data ingestion and preparation stages. It's ideal when dealing with recurring datasets where consistency and efficiency are paramount.

Power Pivot comes into play when relationships in data need to be defined, or when you face analysis that requires extensive summarization across varied dimensions.

The synergy between Power Query and Power Pivot can significantly elevate your analytical capabilities in Excel. By mastering these tools, you not only enhance your productivity but also imbue your projects with a higher level of sophistication and insight. Embrace these functionalities not just as technical skills but as strategic instruments that hone your ability to decrypt data puzzles, revealing not just numbers, but narratives and opportunities hidden within your datasets.

Therefore, as you delve into the nuanced world of Power Query and Power Pivot, envision yourself not just as a user of tools, but as a craftsman in the arena of data. Each dataset tells a story, and with these powerful instruments at your disposal, you're well-equipped to tell it compellingly and with great precision. This mastery over data doesn't just support your current analytical needs but also sets a robust foundation for future, more complex data challenges.

CHAPTER 11: BEGINNER & INTERMEDIATE-LEVEL EXERCISES

Welcome to the practical heart of our Excel journey! By now, you've grasped the fundamentals and dabbled in some advanced features, steering through data management and automation with increasing confidence. As we venture into Day 5, our focus pivots to refining your skills through hands-on exercises crafted for both beginner and intermediate learners. This chapter is designed not merely as a test but as an adventure—a chance to apply your newfound knowledge in scenarios that mirror the challenges of the real world.

Imagine you're at the office, the clock ticking loudly. A project deadline looms, and your boss expects not only accuracy but insights that leap off the spreadsheet. Here, in the safety of our learning environment, you're empowered to simulate those demands. You'll engage in exercises that challenge your ability to format data compellingly, wield formulas with precision, and pivot data to reveal underlying trends—all without the pressure of real-time business consequences.

This chapter breaks down complex tasks into manageable, real-life applications. You'll start by reinforcing your foundation: ensuring your data entries shine with professionalism through impeccable formatting. Next, you'll step up to formula application, addressing common scenarios that you're likely to encounter in an office setting, like summarizing financial reports or analyzing inventory data.

As you advance, the exercises will incorporate some of the more intricate aspects of data sorting, filtering, and basic dashboard creation. It's one thing to learn about a function independently; it's another to see it fit into the larger puzzle of Excel efficiency. The exercises are crafted to bridge this gap, offering you a clearer vision of how various Excel features can streamline tasks and enhance productivity.

By the end of this chapter, equipped with passion and practice, you'll find that what once seemed daunting is now within your command. This isn't just about learning Excel; it's about preparing to excel at whatever challenges come next in your career, armed with the best tools and the confidence to use them effectively.

DATA ENTRY & FORMATTING CHALLENGES

In our continued exploration of Excel, mastering data entry and formatting stands as a pivotal skill that sets the foundation for all subsequent Excel tasks. Whether you're organizing a small dataset or preparing to analyze several thousands of entries, the clarity and precision of your initial data entry and formatting choices have profound effects on the ease of your tasks later.

Here, we'll dive into the nuances of these essential skills, providing clear, step-by-step instructions interspersed with practical, real-world examples. You'll gain not merely an understanding but a mastery of these crucial first steps.

Precision in Data Entry

Every professional journey with Excel begins with data entry. While this might seem deceptively simple, entering data correctly is anything but trivial—it affects everything you do afterwards. The key here is not only understanding how to input data but doing so in a way that anticipates the needs of analysis and reporting later.

1. **Using Excel Tables Wisely:** Start by converting your range of data into a table. Imagine entering sales data. Instead of manually entering each sales figure into individual cells, convert your data range to a table (Ctrl + T). This simple action facilitates features like auto-fill, filtering, and sorting which can tremendously speed up further data operations.

2. **Embrace Data Types:** Excel supports various data types—from basic text and numbers to more complex formats like dates and customized types in newer versions of Excel. For instance, entering a date in the format 'DD/MM/YYYY' enables Excel to understand and process it as a date, rather than as mere string or numeric value. This understanding allows for more powerful operations like sorting by date, calculating durations, and setting up timelines.

Mastering Cell Formatting

Formatting in Excel isn't just about making your spreadsheet pretty; it's about adding layers of meaning and making the data speak.

1. **Number Formatting:** This is crucial when dealing with financial, statistical or technical data. For example, formatting a column of numbers to display in currency format clarifies that those numbers represent monetary values. Similarly, applying percentage format to decimal values instantly transforms them into a more readable and comprehensible percentage format.

2. **Text Alignments and Wraps:** Proper alignment of text can significantly enhance the readability of your data. Headers might be centered to distinguish them from data entries, text within cells might be left-aligned and numbers might be right-aligned as per standard conventions. When dealing with longer text, 'Wrap Text' can be your ally, ensuring that the entirety of the text remains visible by wrapping it within the cell.

3. **Conditional Formatting:** As you dig deeper, making use of conditional formatting can unlock powerful ways of visualizing data directly within the spreadsheet.

   Suppose you're tracking sales data; by setting up conditional formatting rules, you can have all sales above a certain target value automatically highlighted in green, and those below in red. This immediate visual cue can help you spot trends and outliers at a glance.

Effective Data Organization

The power of Excel isn't just in its ability to store data, but to make that data easily navigable.

1. **Customized Data Views:** Freezing panes can help keep heading rows and columns in view while you scroll through the rest of your data, a crucial feature when dealing with expansive datasets.

2. **Splitting Windows:** For comparative tasks, say you're comparing quarterly sales data across two different years, splitting your Excel window to view different sections of your workbook side by side can be incredibly useful. This eliminates the back and forth scrolling, speeding up your analysis process.

Hands-On Practice Exercises

Let's put theory into practice through a series of tailored exercises:

- **Exercise 1:** Create a new workbook and enter data regarding monthly expenses. First, input the data without using tables, then redo the task by converting your data range into a table. Notice the differences in functionality and ease.

- **Exercise 2:** Format a column of numbers representing sales in different regions to currency format. Experiment with alignment options to understand how they affect the presentation and readability of data.

- **Exercise 3:** Set up conditional formatting for a set of performance ratings. Use a color scale to reflect varying performance levels, making the high performers and underperformers instantly recognizable.

By working through these exercises, you not only reinforce your understanding but also enhance your efficiency and readiness to tackle more complex data in real-world scenarios. Remember, these foundations you're building are the stepping stones to advanced data manipulation and analytical tasks in Excel, empowering you to perform at your best in any professional environment.

FORMULA APPLICATION AND TROUBLESHOOTING

In the realm of Excel, formulas are the very sinews that connect mere data to insightful analysis. Grasping the application of formulas and learning how to troubleshoot them when they go awry is akin to learning the secret spells that can unlock the full potential of this powerful tool.

This sub-chapter focuses precisely on that—giving you the strategic know-how to handle formulas like a seasoned pro.

Understanding the Building Blocks

First off, formulas in Excel are built on basic arithmetic—addition, subtraction, multiplication, and division—but their true power lies in their ability to reference cells, perform functions, and automate tasks across large datasets quickly. Every formula starts with an equals sign (=), signaling to Excel that what follows is a calculation.

1. Cell References Are Key: Imagine you're working on a financial report and you need to sum up your monthly expenses. Instead of adding numbers directly in your formula, referencing cells ensure your formulas are dynamic and adaptable to changes. For example, to sum expenses from January to March from cells B2 to B4, you simply use: =SUM(B2:B4). Now, if your expenses change or new expenses are added, your total updates automatically.

Deploying Basic to Complex Functions

2. Simple Summing and Beyond: Starting with simple functions like SUM, AVERAGE, and COUNT, practice drills could involve summarizing daily sales data or calculating average delivery times. As you move to more complex scenarios, such as conditional sums or averages using SUMIF or AVERAGEIF, these become central in analyzing segmented data, like sales by region or customer ratings above a certain score.

3. Handling Dates and Logic: Date functions such as TODAY, DATE, and EOMONTH offer ways to automate entries involving dates. Tasks could include calculating warranties expiry or subscription renewals. Logical functions like IF, AND, OR, not only pose interesting challenge scenarios (e.g., calculating bonuses based on multiple criteria) but hone critical thinking about data.

Troubleshooting Common Formula Errors

Even the best-laid formulas can sometimes lead to errors, which need their own set of detective skills to decode.

4. Debugging Tools: Excel's debugging tools like Formula Auditing can trace precedents and dependents, helping visualize the relationship between cells and the formulas affecting them. This can be crucial when you encounter errors like #VALUE! or #REF!, common culprits being mismatched data types or deleted referenced cells.

5. Logical Troubleshooting: A typical real-world practice could involve resolving errors in profit calculations where you suspect cell references are incorrect. Using F9 to evaluate formula parts or setting breakpoints in more complex calculations can unravel the strands where things go awry.

Practice Scenarios to Build Proficiency

Here's where theory meets the road. Structured exercises not only cement your skills but prepare you for real-world applications.

- **Exercise 1:** Draft a formula to calculate the total annual cost from monthly costs, incorporate conditional formatting to highlight months where costs exceeded the budget.
- **Exercise 2:** Use VLOOKUP to merge customer data from two different sheets, troubleshoot common errors like #N/A which often occur due to mismatches or unsorted data.
- **Exercise 3:** Create a dynamic project timeline using DATE functions and IF statements to indicate task statuses. Extend this by automating email reminders based on task completion status.

In these exercises, not only do you apply the formulas, but you also adjust and troubleshoot them in conditions mimicking the real challenges you will face in a professional environment. Each task is designed to sharpen your toolset, ensuring you not only follow steps but understand how and why certain functions work in specific ways.

By the end of this sub-chapter, armed with both the knowledge of building and troubleshooting formulas, your confidence in handling Excel's formulaic prowess should be solidified. Each formula learned and error resolved adds a layer to your understanding, transforming you from a novice to a proficient Excel user who can harness data to inform decisions smartly and efficiently. Remember, each formula you master is not just a function, but a step towards greater analytical insight and workplace efficiency.

SORTING, FILTERING, AND PIVOT TABLE EXERCISES

Navigating through large datasets in Excel can feel like finding your way through a labyrinth. However, with the right tools and techniques, sorting, filtering, and using pivot tables transform what seems like an overwhelming maze of numbers into structured, comprehensible information that tells a compelling story about the data. This sub-chapter will guide you through practical exercises that solidify your data management skills, using sorting, filtering, and pivot tables to organize and analyze data efficiently.

Taming Data with Sorting and Filtering

Sorting and filtering are your first steps toward making sense of the sea of data. These functionalities help you organize and surface the data that is most relevant to your questions.

1. **Mastering Sorts**: Imagine you have a sales report with hundreds of entries spanning multiple regions and months. Sorting enables you to organize this data alphabetically, numerically, and even chronologically. This functionality isn't just about seeing numbers neatly lined up; it's about quickly spotting trends, like which month had the highest sales, or which region is performing the best.

2. **Deep Diving with Filters**: Filters go a step further by letting you display only the data that meets specific criteria. Suppose you only want to see sales greater than $1,000, or just the entries for a particular region. Filters enable you to hide the rest of the data temporarily. This is incredibly useful when you need to focus on particular segments of data without getting distracted by the full dataset.

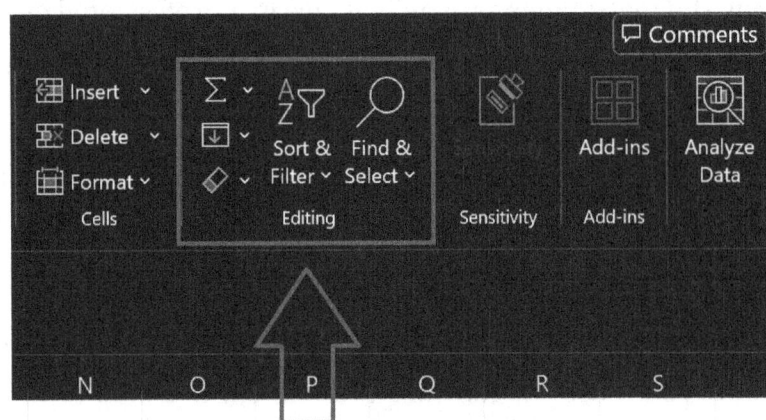

Pivot Tables: Summarizing Data with Precision

Pivot tables are one of the most powerful tools in Excel's data manipulation arsenal. They allow you to reorganize and summarize complex data sets in a table-based format, making it easier to compare and analyze.

1. **Building Pivot Tables**: Consider you have a dataset of national sales for the year, including product types, quantities sold, prices, and regions. A pivot table can summarize this data in seconds. With just a few drags and drops, you can find out which product sold the most across the nation or compare sales performance between regions.

2. **Customizing Pivot Tables**: After creating a pivot table, Excel allows you to arrange the summarized data in various ways. You can choose different aggregation methods like sums, averages, counts, and more.

   You can also filter within pivot tables, focusing the analysis on specific elements. This customization is not just about changing appearances but about deepening the level of analysis.

Hands-On Sorting, Filtering, and Pivot Table Exercises

To embed what you've learned, here are some exercises that simulate real-world scenarios:

- **Exercise 1: Sorting Challenge** - You receive a dataset containing customer feedback ratings (from 1 to 5) along with the date and location of the feedback. Your task is to sort the data first by date (from most recent to oldest) and then by rating (from highest to lowest). This sort order will quickly show you the most recent and highest ratings.

- **Exercise 2: Filtering Data** - Assume you have a staff directory with various departments, employee names, and birthdays. Your goal is to filter the data to show only employees from the "Marketing" department who have birthdays in the current month. This practical use of filtering helps in planning departmental birthday celebrations or rewards.

- **Exercise 3: Creating a Pivot Table** - Using a sales dataset, create a pivot table to calculate total sales per region. Further, enhance the pivot table to compare the average sale per item across different regions. This exercise is crucial for sales managers needing quick insights into regional performance.

- **Exercise 4: Advanced Pivot Table** - Develop a pivot table from a dataset of yearly customer purchases to determine the average spending per customer and categorize it by year and customer loyalty status (new, returning, loyal). This level of detailed analysis can inform customer relationship management strategies and targeted marketing plans.

By working through these exercises, you'll not only reinforce your newfound skills but will also see how effectively sorting, filtering, and pivot tables can turn exhaustive data into actionable insights. Each function you master moves you closer toward becoming proficient in managing and interpreting data, ensuring you are equipped to make informed decisions in any professional setting. Remember, Excel is not just about handling data, but about transforming it into a narrative that supports strategic business decisions.

CHART CUSTOMIZATION AND BASIC DASHBOARD BUILDING

In the digital age where data is king, being able to present that data in a visually compelling manner is crucial. Charts and dashboards not only paint the big picture but also highlight the story that numbers whisper beneath their cold hard surface. This sub-chapter delves into the art and science of chart customization and the basics of dashboard building in Excel, empowering you to transform raw data into insightful visual presentations that communicate effectively.

Understanding Chart Customization

Excel offers a diverse array of chart types—from the classic bar and line charts to more complex radar and waterfall charts. Each chart type serves a unique purpose, so choosing the right one to represent your data is crucial. But it's not just about selection; it's about customization. Tailoring a chart to meet your specific needs can drastically increase its impact.

1. **Choosing the Right Chart**: Imagine you're analyzing annual sales data. A line chart could be perfect for showing trends over time, while a pie chart could help in understanding market share distribution among different product categories.

2. **Customizing Chart Elements**: Once the appropriate chart type is selected, the next step involves refining it by adjusting its elements like titles, axes, labels, and colors. For instance, adding data labels to a bar chart that represents sales figures makes it instantly clear what each bar stands for without having to cross-reference with the axes.

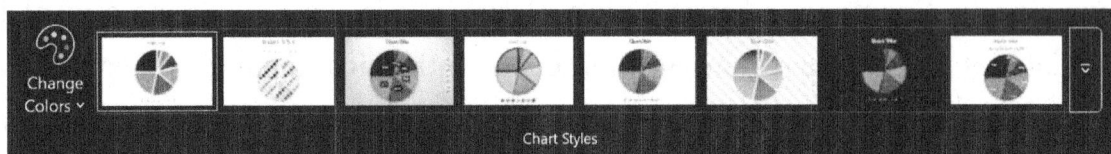

Chart Styles

Building Basic Dashboards

A dashboard in Excel is essentially a visual interface that provides an at-a-glance summary of key business metrics. Effective dashboards are designed not just to display data, but to inform, inspire action, and drive decisions.

1. **Organizing Data**: Before jumping into dashboard creation, it's essential to organize your data. The effectiveness of a dashboard hinges on how well it's fed with organized data. Structuring your data sources efficiently can save countless hours and avoid confusion in the later stages of dashboard setup.

2. **Integrating Multiple Charts**: Dashboards typically integrate multiple charts and tables to provide a multi-dimensional view of the data. For instance, integrating a pie chart showing revenue split with a line chart detailing monthly growth trends can provide a holistic view of performance.

Hands-On Charting and Dashboard Exercises

To turn theory into practice, here's a series of exercises designed to enhance your charting and dashboard skills:

- **Exercise 1: Customizing a Chart** - Create a bar chart using sales data. Customize the chart by adding axis titles and data labels, and adjust the color of bars to differentiate between different years. Focus on making the chart as self-explanatory as possible.

- **Exercise 2: Choosing Charts for Reporting** - Given a set of data types, choose the most appropriate chart types for presenting this data. For example, decide between a line chart and a bar chart when presented with time-series data and categorically grouped data, respectively.

- **Exercise 3: Building a Simple Dashboard** - Using sales and expenditure data, build a basic dashboard. Incorporate a line chart for trend analysis and a column chart for comparison. Include slicers to allow for interactive year-on-year analysis.

- **Exercise 4: Interactive Elements** - Enhance the dashboard created in the previous exercise by adding interactive elements such as dropdown menus and checkboxes. These elements allow users to customize the data they want to see, making the dashboard not just informative but also interactive.

Mastering the creation of customized charts and basic dashboards is integral to translating complex data into straightforward, actionable insights that can influence decision-making processes. Through the practical exercises provided, you are equipped not just with the knowledge of doing so, but with the understanding of how these visual tools can be leveraged effectively in your professional environment. Remember, a well-crafted chart or a well-designed dashboard does more than present data; it tells its story, engaging and informing its audience precisely and effectively.

CHAPTER 12: ADVANCED-LEVEL EXERCISES

Welcome to the summit of your Excel journey—Chapter 12, where your newfound skills are sharpened against the real-world grindstone of business and productivity. Here, we dive into advanced exercises that not only test your mastery of Excel but also prepare you to harness its full capability in sophisticated, impactful ways.

Imagine you're back at work on Monday morning. Your boss hands you a critical project with data so vast it spans multiple spreadsheets, demanding not just analysis but actionable insights within a tight deadline. This scenario isn't just a test of your Excel skills; it's a real-life challenge many face daily. Our exercises in this chapter are crafted to equip you with the prowess to handle such demanding tasks effortlessly.

We begin by replicating complex business scenarios: forecasting market trends, automating financial reports, and managing large datasets that require more than just a surface scratch. Each exercise is designed to be your playground for practicing advanced functions and formulizations you've learned, now applied in a dynamic, unpredictable business environment. From creating powerful macros that automate repetitive tasks to constructing sophisticated dashboards that tell compelling data stories, you are now at a point where Excel becomes more than just software—it becomes a strategic partner in your career.

As we progress, these exercises will challenge you but remember, each step is a building block to an elevated understanding and skill set. You're not just learning; you're becoming proficient in turning raw data into strategic gold. This isn't about getting things right on the first try; it's about iterative learning and growth, ensuring each mistake is a lesson paving the way to expertise.

By the end of this chapter, the term 'advanced' will feel less intimidating and more like a familiar friend. You'll not only stand confidently alongside your Excel-savvy colleagues but also possess the advanced skills to lead, innovate, and transform data into decisions that propel your company forward. So, let's roll up our sleeves and prepare to become not just proficient but powerful users of Excel.

REAL-WORLD BUSINESS CASE SCENARIOS

In the realm of modern business, Excel is not merely a tool; it becomes the very arena where battles for efficiency, clarity, and faster decision-making are won. Advanced users of Excel can maneuver through complex challenges with finesse, turning daunting data sets into coherent strategies. Here, we explore real-world business case scenarios where your advanced Excel skills will stand to test, and triumph.

Financial Forecasting for a Startup

Imagine stepping into the shoes of a financial analyst at a bustling startup. Your task is to forecast the next year's revenues to secure investor confidence and guide internal strategic decisions. With Excel, you apply what you've learned about using FORECAST.LINEAR function which leverages existing data to predict future values.

1. **Gather Historical Data**: Collect monthly revenue data for the past three years. Make sure the data is clean and formatted - continuous dates and corresponding revenue figures.

2. **Set Up Your Forecast Model**: In a new worksheet, create a timeline that extends into the future, matching the historical data's timeline.

3. **Implement FORECAST.LINEAR**: Use this function by selecting your future date cells as the x values and your historical revenues as both y values and known x values.

4. **Analyze and Share Insights**: Generate a line graph to visualize the trend. Share findings with stakeholders using the commenting and share functions in Excel.

By guiding through this process, Excel has not only facilitated a complex analysis with simplicity but also empowered our theoretical analyst to deliver actionable financial insights with confidence.

Optimizing Inventory Management

Consider a retail manager responsible for maintaining the optimal level of stock across multiple stores. Excel's power in data analysis and management comes to the forefront here, specifically through the use of VLOOKUP, pivot tables, and conditional formatting.

1. **Create a Master Inventory List**: This includes stock numbers, supplier details, restock dates, and pricing information.

2. **Deploy VLOOKUP**: Use this to pull in related product data in a sales dashboard providing real-time visibility into which products are under or overstocked.

3. **Set Up a Pivot Table**: This analyzes stock levels across various stores, helping to spot trends and manage reordering schedules efficiently.

4. **Employ Conditional Formatting**: Automatically highlight items that are below minimum stock levels in red, and those that are overstocked in blue, making it easy to identify and correct disparities instantly.

This scenario demonstrates Excel for real-time inventory management, showcasing your ability to keep a lean, efficient supply chain operating smoothly.

Risk Assessment for Market Expansion

An international business consultant evaluates new markets for a company seeking expansion. Using the DATA Table function, they analyze various economic, demographic, and industry-specific variables to forecast potential success.

1. **Prepare the Data Model**: Include variables such as market size, competitive intensity, legal environment, and customer purchasing power.

2. **Utilize DATA Table for Scenario Analysis**: Set up different growth scenarios (optimistic, pessimistic, realistic) and calculate expected impacts on revenue for each.

3. **Incorporate Solver for Optimization**: Use Solver to find the best allocation of marketing budget across different channels for maximum penetration and revenue in the new market.

4. **Visualize with Heat Maps**: Highlight key areas of opportunity and risk visually, facilitating easier comprehension and discussion among strategic teams.

In this case, Excel has enabled the consultant to perform a nuanced risk analysis empowering the business to make informed, data-driven decisions on potential international markets.

Advanced HR Analytics

A human resources manager uses Excel to analyze workforce data to improve employee retention rates. Through combination of INDEX-MATCH, pivot tables, and CORREL functions, they identify patterns and predictors of employee turnover.

1. **Standardize Employee Data**: Gather comprehensive data including department, tenure, performance ratings, and exit interviews.

2. **Analyze with INDEX-MATCH**: Create a dynamic lookup system much more powerful than VLOOKUP, allowing for leftward searches across columns.

3. **Build a Pivot Table for Trend Analysis**: Summarize data to see turnover rates by department and tenure.

4. **Apply CORREL Function**: Identify any strong correlations between department, performance, and turnover rates.

Through these steps, Excel has not only helped to identify retention issues but also enabled the HR manager to devise targeted interventions based on data-driven insights.

Each of these scenarios underscores the transformative potential of Excel when applied to complex, real-world business problems.

Through step-by-step explanations, practical tips, and direct application in concrete examples, you as an advanced Excel user are not just performing tasks; you are actively engaging with data to drive business forward, proving that proficiency in Excel is not just about understanding software, but about envisioning and executing better business strategies.

MACROS & AUTOMATION TASKS

In the ever-evolving workplace, efficiency isn't just an advantage—it's a necessity. One of Excel's most powerful capabilities in driving efficiency is its ability to automate repetitive and complex tasks through macros. Let's dive deep into how you can leverage macros and automation tasks to not just streamline workflows but to reshape them, making your data handling both effortless and error-free.

Envision you're at an insurance company, tasked with processing and updating client records daily—a procedure that perhaps takes several painstaking hours. The transformative potential of macros here is immense, turning what is usually a morning's work into a matter of minutes with just a few clicks.

Understanding Macro Basics

To initiate our journey into automation, first, we need a solid foundation in understanding what macros are: simply, they are recorded actions which can be played back to handle tasks automatically. Whether it's formatting data, generating reports, or importing data, a macro records your actions for future use on repetitive tasks.

1. **Recording a Macro**: The first step in automation is learning to record a macro. Enable the 'Developer' tab in Excel, where you'll find the 'Record Macro' button. Once clicked, every action you take in Excel is recorded—right down to clicking cells or entering data.
2. **Running Your Recorded Macro**: After recording, running your macro is as simple as visiting the 'Macros' dialog box, selecting your macro, and clicking 'Run'. Instantly, all the steps you recorded are replicated exactly.

Streamlining Complex Calculations

Consider the task of monthly sales reporting. Each month, sales data collected needs to be formatted, analyzed, and summarized. Rather than manually adjusting each spreadsheet, you record a macro that formats the sheets, applies necessary formulas, and even creates summary pivot tables.

1. **Set Up Your Data**: Ensure all sales data is consistently formatted. This standardization is crucial so that your macro can be applied effectively across different datasets without errors.

2. **Record the Macro**: Perform the formatting, calculations, and summarizations as you usually would while the macro records your actions.

3. **Edit the Macro for Flexibility**: Once recorded, editing the macro by accessing the VBA (Visual Basic for Applications) editor allows for customization, making your macro robust and adaptable to various datasets.

Automating Data Entry Tasks

For tasks such as data entry, where precision and repetition play significant roles, macros ensure consistency without the fatigue or error rate that might come with manual entry.

1. **Create Templates**: Start with a standardized template for the data being entered. This could be a customer feedback form or a daily sales record.

2. **Record a Data Entry Macro**: As you fill in the template, record these actions. This macro can then be used to ensure each entry follows the same format, reducing errors.

3. **Use Form Controls for Input**: Enhance your template with form controls like drop-down lists or checkboxes, and modify your macro to interact with these controls for even faster data entry.

Handling Complex Automation with VBA

When your automation needs exceed simple recordings, delving into VBA scripting opens up a world of possibilities. VBA allows you to automate virtually any aspect of Excel, from manipulating data and interacting with other applications, to creating custom forms and controls.

1. **Learn Basic VBA Syntax**: Understanding variables, loops, conditions, and procedures is essential. Simple tutorials and practical exercises can rapidly build your competence in VBA.

2. **Debug and Optimize Scripts**: Use the VBA editor's debugging tools to step through your code, verify its correctness, and optimize its performance.

By learning to effectively automate workflows in Excel through macros and VBA, you not only save time but also you scale your proficiency and value in any business setting. Each task automated means more time allotted to strategic tasks—transforming data management from a task you do into a skill that propels your career forward.

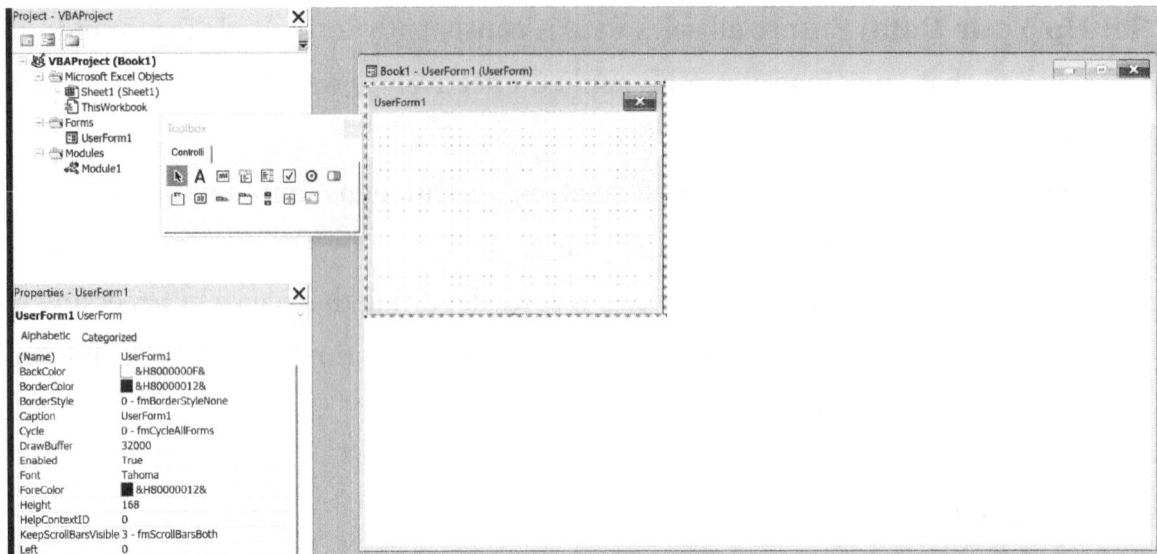

From creating a basic macro to writing a complex VBA script, the journey through Excel automation is both rewarding and enlightening. With each step, you turn from a regular user into an Excel power user, one who knows how to make data dance at the click of a button, ensuring you are not just doing more, but achieving more.

DATA ANALYSIS AND FORECASTING MODELS

In the sphere of business productivity, Excel is not merely a tool for data entry and organization but a powerful ally in predicting and shaping future business outcomes. Through advanced exercises in data analysis and forecasting models, your command of Excel will evolve from basic functional knowledge to a profound capability to foresight and strategy.

Let's embark on a journey where we use Excel to leap from "what is" to "what could be". Here, every number and formula you've mastered prepares you to forecast possibilities, manage risk, and seize opportunities.

Forecasting Market Trends with Exponential Smoothing

Picture this: You're a market analyst tasked with predicting the next quarter's sales trends based on historical data. This scenario needs more than just looking at past figures; it requires understanding the momentum and direction.

1. **Set Up Your Data**: Input your historical sales data sequentially. Ideally, this data should reflect consistent intervals (monthly, quarterly etc.).

2. **Exponential Smoothing**:
   o Utilize the FORECAST.ETS function, which stands for Exponential Triple Smoothing. This function considers not just the trends but also seasonality and pattern changes over time.

- Parameters like the alpha, beta, and gamma control the smoothing level and how much weight is given to recent trends versus seasonal patterns.

By applying this method, you not only get a forecast but a nuanced view of how sales could develop under varying conditions, giving your company the edge to prepare or pivot strategies effectively.

Risk Analysis with Monte Carlo Simulations

Now, assume you're a financial advisor who needs to assess investment risks and returns. Monte Carlo simulations can provide a robust view by forecasting multiple scenarios to see potential outcomes of investment decisions.

1. **Setting Up the Simulation**:
   - Start by defining the possible returns based on historical volatility and expected returns.
   - Use the RAND() function to generate random numbers, which are crucial for creating thousands of probable future states.
2. **Run Iterative Analysis**:
   - Use a loop in VBA to execute the simulation multiple times, capturing the results each time to create a probability distribution of potential returns.
   - Analyze the data to identify not just the most likely outcomes but also the range of potential risks.

This method gives a visual and quantitative foundation to decision-making processes, offering varied strategies based on risk tolerance and market conditions.

Optimizing Supply Chain with Linear Programming

Consider a logistics manager needing to minimize shipping costs while ensuring efficient resource allocation across multiple supply channels. Here, Excel's Solver function is invaluable, utilizing a branch of mathematics known as linear programming.

1. **Define Constraints and Objectives**:
   - List down all constraints, such as shipping capacity, demand, minimum and maximum supply needs.
   - Set an objective, for instance, minimizing costs or maximizing delivery speed.
2. **Utilize Solver**:
   - Set up the Solver parameters to find the optimal solution that meets all constraints.
   - Run Solver, and interpret the output to understand how to best allocate resources across your supply chain networks.

Through linear programming, you transform logistical challenges into streamlined, cost-effective processes.

Predicting Customer Behavior with Logistic Regression

If you're in marketing and tasked with predicting which customers are likely to purchase again or churn, logistic regression in Excel can help predict outcomes based on customer behavior data.

1. **Prep Your Data**: This includes historical data on purchase behavior, customer demographics, engagement scores, and more.
2. **Set Up Logistic Regression**:
   - Use the LOGEST function in Excel for regression analysis. This function can handle binary outcomes (e.g., will buy/won't buy).
   - Analyze the resulting coefficients to understand which factors are most predictive of customer behavior.

This analysis not only predicts future buying behaviors but also helps tailor marketing strategies to customer profiles, increasing ROI on marketing spends.

Through each of these scenarios, your journey with Excel evolves into one where data isn't just what you analyze; it becomes the lens through which you predict and influence future business landscapes. With each exercise, your comfort with complex tools and techniques will grow, turning sophisticated forecasts and analyses into another day at the office fueled by data-driven confidence and strategic foresight.

ADVANCED DASHBOARD & REPORTING EXERCISES

In the high-stakes environment of business intelligence, an advanced dashboard transcends its utilitarian function to become a strategic epicenter where data tells its most persuasive stories. With Excel, crafting sophisticated reporting solutions is not merely about presenting data; it's an art form that combines aesthetics with analytics, transforming raw data into insightful, actionable business intelligence. Let us guide you through the nuances of creating advanced dashboards and reports that can decisively impact business strategies and outcomes.

Constructing the Foundation

Imagine you're tasked with creating a dashboard for a multi-national corporation that tracks key performance indicators (KPIs) across different markets. The goal is to create an interactive tool that senior management can use to get a real-time overview of company performance.

1. **Identifying KPIs**: Start with defining what metrics are crucial for decision-makers. These might include revenue growth, market penetration, customer satisfaction scores, and operational efficiency.

2. **Gathering and Preparing Data**: Consolidate data from various sources—sales databases, customer feedback, market reports, and more. Use Excel's Power Query to clean and structure this data efficiently.

Visualizing Data Through Advanced Charts

Use Excel's varied chart options to create visual representations that not only depict data but also highlight trends, outliers, and progress against goals.

1. **Choosing the Right Charts**: For financial figures, a combination of line graphs and waterfall charts show growth trends and breakdowns of earnings and expenditures. For customer data, pie or doughnut charts can illustrate market segments or satisfaction ratings.

2. **Adding Interactive Elements**: Implement slicers and timeline controls to allow users to filter data dynamically by various dimensions such as time periods, regions, or product lines. This interactivity transforms your dashboard from a static report into an engaging tool.

Leveraging PivotTables for Deep Dives

PivotTables are powerful tools within Excel that allow you to summarize large datasets without writing extensive formulas. They become invaluable in dashboards by providing quick, customizable views into the underlying data.

1. **Configuring PivotTables**: Design PivotTables that executives can use to drill down into specifics, like sales by region or employee performance metrics.

2. **Connecting to Multiple Data Sources**: With Excel's ability to connect directly to external databases, you can set up PivotTables that pull live data, ensuring that your dashboard remains current without manual updates.

Dynamic Reporting with Conditional Formatting

Conditional formatting is a subtle yet powerful way to bring immediate attention to key aspects of your data, such as targets met or missed and anomalies.

1. **Setting Dynamic Rules**: Use conditional formatting to set rules—for example, any sales figures that exceed targets can automatically turn green, whereas underperforming metrics turn red.

2. **Using Data Bars and Icon Sets**: These provide a quick visual summary of performance against benchmarks, adding depth to the data presented.

Automation with Macros

To ensure your dashboard isn't just a one-off report but a continually relevant tool, embed macros that automate data updates and formatting changes.

1. **Writing Macros for Regular Updates**: Create macros that refresh data at a click of a button or on opening the Excel file, saving the need for manual input and reducing potential for human errors.

2. **Scheduling Reports**: Use VBA scripts to schedule automated emails of your dashboard, formatted as PDFs or embedded HTML, ensuring stakeholders receive timely updates.

Advanced Integration

In scenarios requiring real-time data feeds or complex scenarios, integrating Excel with Power BI for enhanced BI capabilities can take your reporting to the next level.

1. **Linking Excel with Power BI**: Streamline the flow from data analysis in Excel to an interactive dashboard in Power BI, where you can exploit robust BI tools and publish reports online for wider access.

Advanced Excel dashboards and reports are not just tools, but mission-critical assets that inform strategies, predict trends, and provide a competitive edge. As you master these aspects of Excel, your role evolves from a data interpreter to a strategic advisor. Through these exercises, you'll find yourself at the juncture where data science meets business acumen, equipped with the skills to lead and inform the future directions of your organization.

Made in the USA
Monee, IL
24 June 2025